Love and Soulmates

Finding Happiness

Albert David Griffith

iUniverse, Inc.
New York   Bloomington

Love and Soulmates
Finding Happiness

iUniverse books may be ordered through booksellers or by contacting:

iUniverse
1663 Liberty Drive
Bloomington, IN 47403
www.iuniverse.com
1-800-Authors (1-800-288-4677)

Because of the dynamic nature of the Internet, any Web addresses or links contained in this book may have changed since publication and may no longer be valid. The views expressed in this work are solely those of the author and do not necessarily reflect the views of the publisher, and the publisher hereby disclaims any responsibility for them.

ISBN: 978-1-4502-1673-9 (sc)
ISBN: 978-1-4502-1674-6 (ebook)

Printed in the United States of America

iUniverse rev. date: 03/25/2010

OF SOULMATES

That at this day love conjugial is so rare as to be generally unknown has been stated several times above. That nevertheless it does actually exist has also been shown in its own chapter, and afterward here and there in those that followed. But apart from that, who does not know that there is such a love, which in delightfulness and excellence so transcends other loves that they all seem to be of small account?

Have there not been, and are there not, those who for the woman desired and solicited as a bride prostrate themselves on their knees, adore her as a goddess, and submit to her as the vilest slaves to her good pleasure? The fact proves that this love exceeds the love of self.

Have there not been and are there not, those who for the woman chosen and solicited as a bride count wealth, yea, treasures if they possess them as nothing and who lavish them also? A proof that this love exceeds the love of the world.

Have there not been, and are there not, those who for the woman chosen as a bride esteem their very life as of no account, and crave death if she does not yield to their petition? A proof that this love is greater than the love of life.

Have there not been, and are there not, those who for the woman chosen as a bride have been made insane by refusal? May not one rationally conclude from this beginning of that love with many, that from its essence this love dominates over every other love as supreme, and at the same time the soul of the man is in it, and promises to itself eternal beatitudes with her who is his choice and solicitation? Who, wherever he may search, can discover any other cause for this than that he has given up his soul and his heart to the one.

For if a lover while in that state were given the option to select the most worthy, the most wealthy, and the most beautiful of all the sex from the universe, would he not spurn the option and hold to his chosen one? For his heart is hers alone.

All this is said so that you may acknowledge that there is a conjugial love of such super-eminence, and that it exists while only one of the sex is loved.

Emanuel Swedenborg

Table of Contents

Foreword

I want to sneak certain very life-improving concepts past your conscious mind into your subconscious mind. I need your cooperation to do that well. If you will not cooperate with me, do not read this book. It will do you no good.

That is because the concepts we are dealing with can only be "known" in nonintellectual ways. You cannot "think" your way into them. You cannot gain their benefits by analyzing them. They must be experienced. For instance, being immensely rich, powerful, famous or influential is of no help at all in acquiring love. The poor, weak, unknown person is on a level playing-field with everybody else where love is concerned.

You can see that it would be impossible to "tell" another person what an orange tastes like no matter how many millions of words you used or how many thousands of books you wrote about the taste of oranges. Yet, you know a simple way to show that person how an orange does taste.

You have him taste an orange.

We are dealing with similar concepts. They are, mainly, love, peace, freedom, and security. I call them "great" gifts. Love actually contains, and is the source of, all great gifts. But the dependent gifts that we name appear to become distinct as our needs and mental states change. Without love, nothing has any real value. Everything is just so much junk for which we find various uses.

Here is how I ask you to cooperate with me in this reading.

Do not think. Read in as much of an intellectually passive state as you can. Thinking causes the conscious mind to become an obstacle, since it "analyzes." Not thinking opens pathways into the subconscious, which, mostly, takes in words very "un-" analytically, very literally.

Then, as you read passively, try to "feel" under and into all words and ideas as they are presented. I wish very much to have you absorb love, peace, freedom and security directly -- as they are -- not as what you "think" they are whenever you think about them.

So, help me to "sneak" love, peace, freedom and security into your deepest inner self by reading along without thought. At the end, do all of the critical thinking that you please. Then decide whether or not anything you have read can be as helpful and rewarding as I truly believe it can be.

A.D.G.

REQUEST

Dear Friend,

Please do not skip this first note. I believe that it is
very important.
Please do not skip anything from now on.
Please do not skim over or speed-read anything. This will give us both
the best chance at what we want. You, to get what I offer. Me, to keep my
promises.
So I ask you to read in a leisurely and receptive way. Because everything
has been chosen and arranged to help you <u>feel</u> certain things. I do not want
simply to put information in front of you.
Accordingly, I ask this: Try to <u>feel</u> what you read. Don't stop and wander
off to think. Try to feel under the words without thinking about them.
I know that you will, finally, need to think about everything here. I know
that you will want to judge my honesty and my character. And you should.
I only ask you to save your hard thinking until the very end. I ask you to
reserve your judgment until the very end, also.
If you do, I feel that you may justly decide upon my honesty, and upon
the kind of person that I am ... at least the kind of person that I want to be.
I do not want this to be just another reading for you. It does not have to
be done in one sitting. Take your time. Read at your own convenience.
But try to <u>feel</u>. Think, only for basic understanding of what the words
<u>seem</u> to mean. Judge when a good judge would. At the end. After the evidence
is in.
Now, please read this page once more.
Thank you.

*Wisdom is
the principal thing;
therefore get
wisdom.*

Happy is the man that findeth wisdom, and the man that getteth understanding.

For the merchandise of it is better than the merchandise of silver, and the gain thereof than fine gold.

She is more precious than rubies, and all the things thou canst desire are not to be compared unto her.

Length of days is in her right hand, and in her left hand, riches and honor.

Her ways are ways of pleasantness and all her paths are peace.

She is a tree of life to them that lay hold upon her, and happy is everyone that retaineth her.

-- Proverbs 3:13

Section One
A Path To Love

Dear Friend,

Everyone wants love.

A person who loves, acts positively toward the world and toward other people. Lovers are the kind people, the philanthropists and saints, the helpful and constructive people.

A person in whom love is absent acts negatively toward the world and toward other people. Among these negative performers are the hateful and destructive people, the psychotics and the psychopaths, the serial killers.

This book is intended to open to love those who do not have it, or to give to those who have love a deeper understanding of it by describing what it really is, which very few people know.

You probably believe that love exists, or, at least, you hope it does.

But there are some people who do not believe in the existence of love. They think that sex, or various kinds of lusts and physical appetites are what give the word "love" its meaning.

It is somewhat worn-out to imply, as we did in the beginning, that each of us is looking for love, but it is probably true that we are. Psychologists like to dilute love down to approval or acceptance, but that is much the same kind of thing.

More people would accept the notion that we are all looking for happiness. That is because we all have some idea of what would make us happy.

In a way, then, this entire book will be about happiness. Especially, about your happiness. And happiness requires love.

No price-tag can be put on love.

No doubt you see that wealth is less valuable than health. The proof is that many persons willingly part with their last dollar to try to be free of sickness.

Similarly, you cannot put a money value on love. First, you cannot go out and buy it directly. Second, if you had it, you could not sell it to someone else even if you wanted to.

But priceless love may be the source and support of other gifts, including health and wealth.

If you were able to begin to bring such gifts into your life in this reading, what price would you agree to pay? And would it not be worth the effort?

So now, for the purposes of this reading, let us agree that love is real -- that it is possible to be happy.

But, if you will not grant that, at least grant this. That there is something you are looking for -- something, perhaps unknown, that you wish would come and make your life more satisfying.

Your aim is to find that priceless, most satisfying "something." My aim is to help you find it.

This writing is a chance to look further for it.

That something, does exist.

No one of us lives long enough to have all the different experiences that make the job of finding happiness easier. That is why we each need outside helps like this book. Such aids extend our understanding of how best to meet life from day to day, because they can gather into one place the testimonies of thousands of people over thousands of years.

One short lifetime gives us very little in experience to answer some of the questions we often discuss so glibly: Does God exist? How did the world come to be? What is matter? Worse, we let arguments about such questions keep us from using some of the rules of life that all traditions agree upon as being ways to find happiness.

Part of the intention of this book is to give you a way to "sidetrack" those questions, and the arguments about them, long enough that you will have a chance to bring some of the good results of all human experiences into your daily life.

One of our beginning points was that you might not have love and its attendants gifts, and that you want them. In any event, they are desirable, and if you did not desire them, you would not read this book.

And that you desire love and its gifts should be the <u>only</u> reason you read this book.

You are not asked to read this book because of some "authority" or a religion or a religious text or a religious leader. Right now, <u>you</u> are the only "authority."

But, soon, I will ask you to find your own name for whatever you think might be the central "power" that makes everything happen in the world. I will also offer some suggestions as to how you might do that.

When you have decided upon your own name for that *power*, or borrowed a name to suit yourself, <u>that</u> power will be the only authority you need to consider.

Then, because <u>you</u> have chosen the name for "the power" in this world, YOU will be the only AUTHORITY in this search to find your own way to be happy.

So this approach to obtaining the gifts of which we desire the benefits will be unique to you. And I believe that this approach is different from most other approaches.

This approach is also different from other approaches because it does not insist that you meet certain preconditions, such as those implied by the following statements.

1. You do not, at first, need to be moral or good, in the everyday sense of those words, to benefit from the "ways" of acting that will be described later.

2. You do not, at first, need to be unselfish to be rewarded in a meaningful fashion by gaining the gifts we discuss.

3. You do not, at first, need to do good "from the heart" to enjoy the rewards of doing good.

4. You do not, at first, need to "have faith," in the ordinary sense, to use the "codes of conduct" reviewed here and benefit from them.

5. You do not, at first, need even to "believe," in the ordinary way to use "the power" and make your life happier.

6. You do not, at first, need to "understand" why the rules to be given work for you. You can use them without understanding them. There are many, many, concepts and procedures that we use every day which work and which we do not understand.

The point is, you do not have to have undergone any kind of religious or meditational training, no sort of "purification" to understand and be "fit" to receive the love of which we speak.

Because, making love real is not an intellectual or meditational process. You cannot be lectured into love or into becoming loving. Words and thinking have nothing to do with receiving and internalizing love. So do not read anything that is written here as if it were a lecture, or as if I were just trying to "tell" you something.

But words can be used as a kind of "Trojan Horse" to bypass the brain. And that requires you to try to "ignore words," insofar as you can.

Which, in turn, requires that you "feel" words without thinking about them.

Most importantly, you must try to feel "under" words, as you read them.

That is how to use words as Trojan Horses.

Finally, it is important to read everything here, <u>slowly</u>, without skipping ahead or skimming. Do not stop to "figure" anything out. Then this will not be just another book read randomly.

"Understanding" has nothing to do with trying to get to what we want, here.

If you say you "must understand," you will get stuck in arguments with yourself about science, philosophy, and religion. Such arguments will stand between you and the "feel" you need to be open for.

I do not argue for any particular church or religion or human or mystical school. Churches, "schools" or similar entities are brought in only to see what they all agree on. You will then begin to get the "feel" that comes with love and its attendant gifts. That "feel" is also part of the special reality out of which love and its gifts come. (We will examine a view of that "reality" later.)

So, please, read, and try to "feel" <u>under</u> the words.

Section Two
Of Soulmates

Here is how it is.

Love comes into us somehow.

The luckiest person is one whom love seeks out.

The second luckiest person is the man who meets the sole (the only possible) woman who actually completes him. He and she will both experience the unitizing love that results.

I am that second kind of person.

Now, bear with me while I tell you just a little about myself and my "love" experience. Then you should see why I am trying to help you to, after your own fashion, "feel out" for love rather than to try to grasp it either physically or intellectually.

Up to 1967, I was a sceptic in my approach to everything. I wanted to learn all there is to know. I read widely, attended college, studied philosophy, and got a Bachelor of Arts degree.

I thought that if any question could not be handled by Science, it was not worth any time. I talked as if I could not know whether there was such a thing as the soul, or a God. I was, by label, an agnostic.

But in my heart I felt there was nothing like a soul, or a God, or anything real behind such concepts. So, in my thinking, I was really an atheist. (This is one reason I suspect that all who call themselves agnostics are atheists in practice.)

For me, then, (and for most <u>educated</u> or "professionally" <u>smart</u> people) there was only a world of <u>matter</u> to deal with.

The problem, with matter, is to explain how things like "mind," "values," and "feelings" can come out of something which has the qualities that matter is said to have. Matter is defined as having mass, inertia, form, height, width, and depth. Mind, values, and feelings are not defined in material terms anywhere that I have heard of.

Besides, no materialist could explain how matter came "to be" in the first place. But that did not bother me. It did not seem to bother any materialist.

Isn't that strange?

Materialists know only a "ghost" of matter.

It is bad enough that the materialist does not know how matter came to be. But this is worse: He does not even know what matter is.

So, if, 1, the materialist cannot account for mind, values and feelings; or, 2, cannot explain how matter came to be; and, 3, does not even know what matter is: he is totally ignorant of all of the absolutely basic facts he needs in order to know truth <u>in his own</u> terms. All that the materialist can do is use his imagination about those three essentials. And, in Science, imagination is not accepted as a means to establish truth.

The materialist system, then, is based upon nothing better than a "ghost." The system is made of the materialist's "imaginings" about matter. Again, it is a kind of ghost of matter.

How can a materialist system have any meaning if it contains no explanation of what matter is? What the materialist calls matter could be anything else. He merely guesses about what matter is and then describes matter in terms of his guesses.

See what Will and Ariel Durant say about the nature of matter in their History of Civilization, Volume IX, The Age of Voltaire, Chapter XXI, The Spreading Campaign; end of chapter:

"As to matter having the power to generate life and mind, Voltaire, though he too had once inclined to that view, preferred a modest agnosticism to d'Holbach's (Holbach, Paul-Henri Dietrich, baron d') confident assumptions:

['Experience (Voltaire quotes from the Systeme) proves to us that the matter which we regard as inert and dead assumes action, life, and intelligence when it is combined in a certain way.'

But this is precisely the difficulty, (says Voltaire.) How does a living germ arise? Of this, the author and the reader are alike ignorant. Hence, are not the System of Nature, and all the (philosophical) systems in the world, so many dreams?

It would be necessary (says d'Holbach) to define the vital principle, which I deem impossible.

Is not this very easy? (Voltaire responds) ... Is not life organization with feeling? But that these two properties can arise solely from matter in motion it is impossible to prove; and if it is impossible to prove, why afffirm it? ... Many readers will feel indignant at the decisive tone assumed when nothing is explained....

When you venture to affirm that there is no God, or that matter acts of itself by an eternal necessity, you must demonstrate this like a proposition in Euclid; otherwise you rest your system on a 'perhaps.' What a foundation for a belief that is of the greatest importance to the human race!]

.... In Germany it was d'Holbach's materialism, as well as Hume's skepticism, that aroused Kant from his 'dogmatic slumber.' Perhaps Marx through devious channels inherited his materialistic tradition from d'Holbach.

Long before the Baron wrote, Berkeley had made the most damaging point about materialism: mind is the only reality directly known; matter (since d'Holbach defined it as 'all that affects our senses') is known only indirectly, through mind: and it seems unreasonable to reduce the directly to the indirectly known....

We are not so clear about matter as we used to be; we are as much mystified by the atom as by mind; both are being resolved into forms of energy that we cannot understand.

And it is as difficult now as in the days of Locke and Voltaire to imagine how 'matter' can become idea, much less consciousness.

The mechanistic interpretation of life proved fruitful in physiology, but the possiblity still remains that organs (matter) may be products and instruments of desire (mind), like the muscles of an athlete."

(End of quote from The History of Civilization.)

I, the author, then, had always seen all arguments from the side of matter. I accepted that physics, chemistry, and other sciences would "someday" explain how love and duty and honor come out of matter as the scientists defined it.

I even believed that love was basically sex. Maybe because this is a common idea, supposed to have come out of Freud, but which did not.

However, no psychologist or psychiatrist that I know of defends the idea that love and sex are the same. Psychologists do not do a very good job, though, of explaining what they mean by love or how it arises from the physical situation.

But they generally believe that it is one thing to want to have sex with someone, and another thing to love that person. Sex and love can go together. Ideally, they should. But they often do not. Many couples have sexual intercourse who do not love each other. And many couples love each other who do not have sexual intercourse.

No matter, up to 1967 I thought I had a fair idea of what love was. When I was four years old I knew a pretty girl in her teens. I can still remember the delight and warm joy I felt whenever I could be with her. I took flowers to her and visited her. I could not do much about my feelings, now knowing what to do. But if you take the common experience which we call love, I have no doubt that that is what I felt. I could not, very confidently, at only four years of age, have attached the name to my feelings. But I "knew" love whether or not I could put the label on it.

I experienced the same feeling for other girls, over the years. Sex was never involved. Simply holding hands and sharing contentment was tremendously pleasing and satisfying. I, and many of you, would call that "love enough," and want no more. Many of us settle for this limited state of shared passion, and must do so.

But love can be much more.

And we come to "ROMANCE."

I, just as you probably have, did read stories, and often dreamed of the good and kind and beautiful heroines in them. These ladies seemed to be something I should look for, and I did.

When I was in eighth grade, a person in the class made me feel she was such a girl. From then on, although I was too shy to tell her, she was my ideal on earth, and remained so for more than twenty years.

In 1949 I got married. By 1967 my wife and I had three nearly-grown children. I still accepted that the closest one could get to love, in real life, was to have sex.

And all this time I was a sceptical materialist, agnostic in mind, and atheistic in heart. The most that I could see as being vaguely ideal in the world were the strong desires I had experienced for the young ladies I have mentioned.

But in 1967 I was exposed to the presence and passive influence of a young woman who affected me much differently than any had done before. First, and most obviously, she was outstandingly beautiful. Everyone who saw her, thought so. To me, she was the most beautiful thing that ever was or ever will be.

But what most intrigued me was the growing conviction that she was another <u>me</u>; that she was internally exactly the same sort of person as I was. She behaved as I did, and appeared to have the same ways of interacting with other people.

And others could see these similarities. One of our co-workers even said, in commenting upon this: "My god, another Griffy!"

Which brings us to the concept of "soulmates." And the bridge is, that I came to feel that the young woman was entirely like me. I had never felt like this about any girl, desiring sex or not. I had never felt that any man, even, was so much like me. Besides, I would not have thought that such a sameness was possible between me and another human. I had never identified that way with anyone I was ever fond of.

So I was convinced that this girl and I were really one person in some way -- that each of us was, somehow, a sort of half. (Remember, scientists maintain that male and female organisms originated from a single, neutral sort of primordial cell.)

(I learned, after this experience, that there is a romantic or mystical legend called the "doctrine of soulmates." The doctrine says that each of us has one, and only one, matching half of him- or herself in a member of the opposite sex. Further, that each of us longs to be with that person if we are not. Because, as long as these matching, one and only, halves are apart, each will feel uncomfortably incomplete.)

Can such a relationship of halves be explained in material terms? (I ask, because I am not trying to convince you of anything, just now, I am simply trying to make a long story short. You will need to decide, yourself, where truth lies, after you have reviewed all that follows this introduction.)

Please note that my belief that my unique love and I were one creature in some nonphysical fashion did not involve intellectual conviction. I accepted without question that our unity was a fact, and that it could be explained only in spiritual terms. Because I had always ridiculed such terms, I was in an awkward position to explain my new feelings and beliefs.

Which forced me to this question: What is science good for? It was obvious that science was of no use concerning soulmates.

Science has no explanations for a spirit life. Science even sees itself as having no tools to prove or disprove spiritual questions.

We will see later that science cannot even explain the strongest feelings that we all have. Indeed, it is difficult to get some scientists to admit that we experience such feelings at all, in spite of the fact that they feel them, too.

How <u>do</u> you account for the feelings we have? What is going on when we feel hate, or fear, or love? Psychologists like B. F. Skinner want to ignore the realness and meaning of emotions in organizing life and deciding the worth of things. They want to dismiss emotions from consideration, clinically, which in practice is much the same as saying that they do not exist.

The point is, science was of no use to me in analyzing this area of internal <u>knowing</u> that I had entered into.

I now believed that my felt unity with my soulmate could be explained only in terms of spirit. What most convinced me of this was a strong "will to do" within me when before I had always been a watcher and waiter. Also, the process of the girl and I coming to know each other had seemed to take care of itself. Our private meetings were easy to arrange, and always positive and peaceful.

This relationship ended after three months. I came out of it believing that I was correct in seeing the young woman as so much like me. We were, and are, one creature, even if not now together. And we had not damaged any third party. We had only accepted and understood each other.

It seemed to me that some "power" had taken care of everything.

Some power "not of this world" had brought me and my soulmate together, I believed. Too much had been done for me when I was at a complete loss over what to do. Too many "values" and "ethical factors" had invisibly prevented unacceptable interractions between the girl and me.

I certainly wanted a much closer relationship. But a conviction arose in me that a higher law, if broken, would destroy any possibility of the happy association that I longed for. I was not about to take a chance on that.

The world could no longer be "material" to me. The idea that matter, as materialists and scientists talk about it, could give rise to the feelings and "worths" I came to realize with this young woman who was such a revelation to me was ridiculous. That notion seemed much more ridiculous than the idea that there was a soul, a spiritual life and a God had seemed before.

Science had no term at all to touch the reality of the inside world I had found. Nor could that world be explained away with the crazy language of the behaviorists. Science in general, and psychology in particular, have little time for that reality. Psychologists and psychiatrists, mostly, consider God to be part of the imagination of some of their patients. But they often calculate that if something in the "idea of God" keeps the patient stable or helps him to make good decisions, then that idea of God can be an acceptable part of treatment.

Science, then, to repeat, was of no use to me in handling the internal forces which I felt. Science could not deal with those forces in idea. Science could not define their reality.

What did that mean?

It meant that science was not to the point. Science could not say how I "feel" forces like that. But, feel them, I did, and do. Science could not say what the reality of such forces was. But real they were and are, because I felt them and feel them.

You feel those forces, too. And you do not have to be a scientist to "know" that they are real.

The world was spiritual. I was convinced. If it was not spiritual, then it was certainly not material in the sense that you and I are practically forced to believe every day by pressure from the "outside."

I had had a "conversion experience." It was not a "dramatic" or sudden one. It had lasted too long. Three months. I had been able to observe it too well. But it was complete. And it brought with it all of the elements that a real conversion experience is supposed to bring. That is the test.

(We will look at some examples of the sudden or dramatic conversions of other people later.)

What about the "power?"

If one accepts the opinion put forth in Will Durant's History of Civilization that sensory phenomena are more "direct" than the apparently "external things" of which our senses inform us, then the sensory phenomena <u>are</u> "more real" than the external things.

At least, I felt I had had direct experience of a power I had not known before. I was convinced that whatever that power was, it was the same as what we call "love," whenever love is considered to be separate from sex.

But name the "power," yourself. Call it electricity, or magnetism, or "whatever you please," that will be your title for the "force" that keeps the world going.

What you have named, or will name, is the only source of "real" meaning, of all motion, of all sensation, in our lives.

The experience made me feel that I did "know" <u>love</u> as the inner power.

So I had <u>love</u>.

And love brought me peace. I did not have any answers. But I had no questions.

I was at <u>peace</u>.

Chains of every kind had dropped from me. I had been set free.

I was <u>free</u>.

Love made me feel there was nothing more that I had to be afraid of.

I was <u>secure</u>.

I came to see love, peace, freedom, and security as four great gifts.

Over periods of six months to three years, I gained all four of those gifts. Not as strongly at first as later. The gifts need to grow. They need to be cultivated. They must be weeded. Emotional and "idea" weeds have to be kept out of them, and pulled from among them.

The four gifts came to me as they are listed. Love, peace, freedom, and security, in that order.

My soulmate is not now with me. But out of my experience with her came those gifts. And they can never be taken from me.

So what?

Am I suggesting that you go out and search for your soulmate; that you involve yourself in a series of romances in the hope that you will come across the source of the four great gifts that way?

No.

The path will be your own. You will have your own kind of experience. It may or may not be an experience of love, as such. The thing experienced may be something that you will call by another name. We cannot say what <u>you</u> will experience.

Whatever happens, when it happens, you finally will "know" what all kinds of valuable phrases really mean. You will know what the phrase, "If the son of man set you free, ye shall be free indeed," means <u>in experience</u>. <u>Not</u> because you <u>understand</u> it, but because <u>you have</u> such freedom.

You will understand many other phrases in the same way. <u>Not</u> in your head. In your heart. There are thousands of precious sayings into which most people never get insight, never "see into." They try to <u>think</u> them. That can't be done.

You have heard many such sayings: "There is no fear in love, but perfect love casteth out fear." "Ye shall know the truth, and the truth shall make you free." "He who is first shall be last, and he who is last shall be first. "God is love." "The letter of the law killeth, but the spirit giveth life." "He who knows does not say; and he who says does not know."

You will "know" what "The Holy Grail" is, and "The Philosopher's Stone," and "the pearl of great price," because you will have <u>found</u> them. (Actually, you will have found <u>IT</u>. Those three concepts are all one and the same.)

Then you will aim rightly in everything that you do, even when you "can't think." Because in finding "the pearl of great price," you will "automatically" become "one-pointed," in the sense in which mystics talk about it. Or, as The Bible has it: "If thine eye be single, thy whole body shall be full of light."

We will leave such concepts, for now. But when you become truly "one-pointed," you will begin truly to "know yourself."

And you will develop an uncommon way of "knowing."

All that you come to "know" about phrases like those given before will work for you in this material life. It will work for you exactly as in the spiritual life, or, if you wish, in your emotional life.

All of this you will begin to "know," or to "know better," if you will feel your way through this whole reading and do not "pick at things." Don't argue with yourself or with anyone else about what you read.

You will feel into a "grab-bag."

You will see, along the way, some medical opinions and some examples of dramatic conversions. You will see samples of ethical and religious writings. Of poems.

If you give your attention and your cooperation to everything as I have suggested; that is, by trying to "feel" what you read, you can more easily gain the benefits of love which you seek.

Back to having you name "The Power," as I before asked you to do.

Confirm, now, whether or not you have any name for "the power" that keeps the world which you see, changing and moving every day. For the world, obviously, does move and change, constantly.

And some force or power has to keep it moving and changing.

If you do not have a name of your own to give the "power," choose one. I will list some that have been used. You may discover others elsewhere. I do not care what your choice is. But it must "set well" with you. You name it.

Some terms that you might use "on trial," are: Gravity. Love. God. Magnetism. Energy. Vibration. Cosmic Force. "The Force," as in "Starwars." "The Power." Consciousness. The Vital Essence. Material reality. Universal Mind. Intelligence.

Or any name you choose.

But, again, try to <u>feel</u> through, with me.

I will not <u>describe</u> the series of feelings which I had in the changes that brought me the four "great gifts."

I will try to <u>give</u> you, or try to <u>cause you to "feel,"</u> the same series of "feelings" I had in the changes that brought me love, peace, freedom, and security.

You <u>must</u> try to feel them. Do not think them. Where I believe it will be useful for you to have a theory in mind, I will offer one, and tell you why. Please accept such theories at the times they are offered. Then, there is more chance that your "instincts," or intuition, will sense certain "answers," and you will "know" them.

Remember: READ SLOWLY FROM THE PREFACE TO THE VERY END OF THE LIST OF BOOKS WITHOUT SKIPPING. Use as many sittings as you need for your own "slow speed." Please <u>do</u> be "slow." Better too slow than too fast.

And: READ ALONG AND TRY TO UNDERSTAND WHAT EACH WORD <u>SEEMS</u> TO MEAN, BUT DO NOT STOP TO TRY TO FIGURE OUT THE MEANING OF ANY OF THE IDEAS. Stay away from the dictionary until the next time through.

So, try to be open-minded and "feel" instead of "think," this first time you read the book. You may find some of the reading boring, but even what is boring should be rewarding.

Section Three
Try To Feel

This is repetition. At this beginning, it is important to put "feeling" before thinking. But this time, let us add some suggestions.

While you read, <u>do not</u> make any <u>decision</u> about the truth or falsity of any particular, passing statement. But, while you read, <u>do decide</u> whether or not you see any <u>use</u> in what you read. Also, decide if you could try any of the suggestions, yourself, as experiments. (It is understood that you will keep your own beliefs about what is real and not real unless you see some reason to change those beliefs.)

The preceding considerations are important. The question is not whether or not you can bring yourself to accept any of the reasons for what I say you should do. The question is, "Could you <u>use</u> the material and the suggestions?" Try only to answer that.

Why? To get love, the most valuable thing in the world, and its attendant gifts: peace, freedom, and security.

Remember to consider using, in your own way, some of my suggestions whenever they are given.

Because, if I were to go into too much detail in describing my own feelings and what actually happened to me as love and its gifts came to me, my views would be too "spiritual" or too "religious" for many people, and I want to avoid such a barrier.

For that reason, I wish to make it clear that whatever I ask you to try will work whether you are "religious" or "spiritual" or not. They will work for an atheist. They will work for an agnostic. They will work for the so-called "smart" person, and the so-called "dumb" person.

Again, to repeat, focus only on <u>what is to be done</u>. Put aside, for a while, <u>what you think</u> about what is to be done.

Now, let us assume the following to be true: That good behavior brings one rewards, and that bad behavior brings one penalties.

I hope you believe that you should help your fellow men. But even that is not, right now, a <u>necessary</u> belief. I am depending upon your wish to be happy. I trust, since you wish to be happy, that you will <u>test</u> ways to bring love, peace, freedom, and security to you -- so that you will be happy after the manner you desire. That desire ought to cause you to test the "ways" or "codes" just as I present them. If not, you may have strong reasons of your own to test any codes presented.

How do you look at things?

Consider whether or not the following idea might be true.

It is not so important how things <u>are</u> in our lives, but how we <u>look</u> at things.

Assume, for purposes in reading this book, that that idea is true: That how we look at things in our lives may be more important than how things actually are. You need not agree that that is true. Simply treat it as I ask you to treat any quotation I present: as a possible way of looking at reality -- at what is real and what is "of worth."

Remembering that we are trying to contrast the effects upon ourselves of "how we look at things" as opposed to reacting to "how things actually are," let us examine some of the concepts within the "grab-bag" of ideas that we referred to before.

These ideas are from a variety of sources: from psychology and psychiatry; out of Chinese philosophy; from The Bible. There are some quotes from medical doctors, reflecting practice, or from books on experimental physiology. Other quotations are from our own, Western, philosophy. All of the quotes are easy to understand. But I ask you, again, to read the material with an open mind, and, perhaps, intuition.

At the moment, I am <u>not</u> asking you to believe that there is a God. I believe that there is one, I have said why I do, and I will present some additional observations which I think support that belief. But, also again, you do not have to believe that God exists in order to successfully use my method of gaining the "great gifts."

Humans go to a lot of trouble to discover the "laws of nature." You and I know that we should not go against those laws. We learn that it is easier to work with them. You learn to line your "self" up with nature's laws.

What is that "self?"

In psychology, a conscious, everyday self is recognized. Someone may yell out to you, "Hey, you!" The self he calls to is that everyday self.

But an unseen self exists deeper within you than that everyday, or outside, thinking self. This inner self gives much of the "push" to our everyday thinking. It is also the place most of our dreams come from.

And that deeper self "records" everything we have ever felt, tasted, smelled, heard, or seen -- in all our lives. Everything. That self never forgets anything. Science has fairly well demonstrated that the record there is that complete.

For that reason, partly, I ask you, for now, to accept that that inner self is a superman. He keeps all of the records. He is much stronger than you are, as you know yourself, outside. (Note: I did not say that you should believe this. I asked you only to accept it "for now." If you are not, so, temporarily accepting, you may not "see" some later thinking.)

Often, you find out about that inside man when you have feelings you can't explain. You may be frightened, and not know why. Certain people may irritate you excessively, and you may not know the "why" of that. You may like someone without knowing why, not care for someone else, with as little apparent reason. You may feel yourself to be worth less or worth more than some other person, in the same, unexplainable way.

You may say, "I wish I could figure out what is 'bugging' me." Well, whatever is bugging you, or "eating on you," is really bugging or eating on that inside superman. You, as your outside self, can only fight with whatever is doing the bugging as well as you can.

And your feelings can affect your body.

There are two sets of nerves in the body. One set is the one you use to "get around" and "do" whatever you do. The other set is the "more inside" set, which works itself. This inside set of nerves makes most of our emotions.

A Canadian doctor, Hans Selye, studied how the body changes in disease. He concluded that in disease, the body is in "stress," and that this stress throws the body's chemistry out of balance.

Dr. Selye's "stress picture" of disease is now widely accepted in medicine. This stress picture shows what happens in <u>every</u> disease. In every disease, a definite complex of chemicals is let out of affected tissues into the blood. These chemicals are of the histamine group. They cause most of the pains and body changes found in any disease.

Certain strong emotions can cause the production of discomfiting histamines, too. Dr. Selye said that when you feel hate, fear, envy, jealousy, or spite, or meanness, these are so-called "bad" emotions. At least, they are bad for the body, because of the adverse effects of the histamines on us.

So, those feelings can cause you to be sick. They do damage, just as a cut or a burn damages a hand or a foot. Such feelings are "bad" for the body just as a "wrench in the gears" is bad for a machine. Your body can be killed bit by bit by stress in the same way that it can be by physical blows or falls. It may just take longer. But it may, at times, kill quickly.

You may say, then, that bad emotions equal bad health. And you may say, as justifiably, that good emotions equal good health.

Dr. Selye also said that other emotions -- in which you feel cheerful, calm, contented, lucky or brave, and so on -- make chemicals in the body, too. But these feelings produce "good" chemicals.

Both the good and the bad chemicals work through a gland in your head, the pituitary gland. Still, the bad chemicals make you sick, and the good chemicals help you to stay well.

For that reason, it is possible for you to regulate your own body-chemistry for the better.

If "good feelings" are brought in and kept in being as much as possible, they "kill off" the harmful chemicals that cause disease. The good feelings or emotions work through the pituitary gland to keep body chemicals "right." And when you keep good feelings, your body "gets itself" healthy, and stays healthy.

You can keep your feelings more right than wrong by being active at things you like to do, and being with people you like to be with. If you cannot be active, yourself, for any reason, you may bring active people to you, or be taken to them.

Or, more easily, you may read, or be read to, out of the very many different kinds of writings that tell you why you should feel well and be optimistic. That is one reason I have added a list of books to this material.

A mechanism of "Crime and Punishment" may be thought of in picturing the back-and-forth motions of good and bad chemicals in your body.

I earlier said that the main idea in this entire book is, "that good behavior is rewarded, and bad behavior is punished."

That idea is hardly more than "common sense." It has been so presented by many good writers.

John E. Gibson wrote such an article in the "Family Weekly" of September 22, 1974. He handled very well the concepts which we are considering, like this:

Mr. Gibson begins by presenting a choice.

TRUE OR FALSE: People who practice the Golden Rule are healthier than those who don't. [(See number 2 (of 5 statements.)]

TRUE OR FALSE?

1. Nobody can really define what "being good" is. Behavior that is termed "good" by one person may be labeled "bad" by another -- there are no fixed standards to go by.

2. People who practice the Golden Rule are healthier than those who don't.

3. If you're insincere in your dealings with others, you have a good chance of becoming paranoid.

4. The good die young.

5. Science cannot explain why some people seem to be more subject to accidental mishaps than others.

ANSWERS

[(1.) Nobody can really define what being good is.]

1. *False.* "Being good" is defined succinctly by behavioral specialists thusly: It consists of doing to your fellow-men as you would be done by; of keeping on speaking terms with your conscience; and of doing the best you can to bridge the distance between your *actual* self and your *ideal* self -- the kind of person you'd like to be. As one psychologist has observed in formulating a yardstick for virtue, "It's pretty hard to be a louse and practice the Golden Rule at the same time."

[(2.) People who practice the Golden Rule are happier than those who don't.]

2. *True.* People who practice the Golden Rule have fewer colds, digestive upsets, headaches -- and are less subject to all types of serious ailments and diseases. Medical studies conducted at the National Institutes of Health, Cornell Medical Center and elsewhere have shown that people who are the least subject to illness tend to differ markedly from others in that they are more concerned with the welfare of others, more trusting of others, more charitable of people's faults, more outgoing in their general outlook on life. Personality tests showed that they are more at peace with themselves and easier to get along with. It was also found that when people in this category did become ill, they averaged a far speedier recovery time.

[(3.) If you're insincere in your dealing with others, you have a good chance of becoming paranoid.]

3. *True.* A wide-scale psychological study of the personalities of men and women of various temperaments showed that persons who were evasive and deceptive in their dealings with others were significantly more fearful than those who were sincere and forthright. Other studies have shown that when someone is dishonest, his self-esteem suffers and he becomes unhappy with himself. And a person who is unhappy with himself, psychologists point out, tends to be suspicious and distrustful of the actions of others -- that is to say, paranoid.

[(4.) The good die young.]

4. *False.* People who sincerely try to do their best and who are considerate in their relations with others average much longer lives. Sociological studies at Johns Hopkins University and at the University of Pittsburgh show that such a person is far less likely to die in a traffic accident than someone who is habitually belligerent, loud-mouthed or otherwise socially obnoxious. The good-living individual has also been found to be much less subject to other types of accidental injuries.

[(5.) Science cannot explain why some people
seem to be more subject to accidental mishaps
than others.]

5. *False.* Studies show that latent guilt feelings are a basic cause of accident-proneness. The individual who suffers them seeks consciously or unconsciously to assuage his conscience by self-punishment -- either by "forgetting" to take ordinary precautions in his everyday comings and goings or by exposing himself to unnecessary hazards.

That concludes Mr. Gibson's article.

So, medical research appears to confirm that the varying feelings which we experience directly and demonstrably affect our bodies. If you feel too much anger, envy, spite, fear, and other such emotions, you bring upon yourself illness and pain. If you feel love, optimism, acceptance, are helpful, and wish well to yourself and to others around you, you are rewarded by health, comfort, and feeling good.

This rule of reward and punishment is true in everything. It is true in the body. It is true in the emotions. It is true in the mind and spirit. It is true in the smallest things and in the largest.

And, very importantly, please note the following.

Within the body, the reluctance of any one of us to be bound by "rules" of "right and wrong" is beside the point. Reluctant or not, even very unwilling, we sink or we swim, in health, by the effects of those rules.

This brings us back to the four great gifts.

You want love, peace, freedom, and security. You would be quite strange if you did not. You would want health, too. Possibly, wealth.

Health and wealth have no <u>necessary</u> connection to love, peace, freedom and security. But you gain, and keep, good health, insofar as you learn to love, be at peace, and be free, and secure. You can, then, more easily gain love, peace, freedom and security if you avoid feeling hate, anger, envy, and the other "bad" emotions.

But it is difficult to go <u>directly forward</u> upon the path of controlling one's emotions. So let's explore an easier route.

Let's try to understand "happiness."

You may have noticed that we have not talked about happiness so far. And we started out by saying, among other things, that this entire book was actually about <u>your</u> happiness.

But we did not talk so directly about happiness, itself, because it depends, for its own being, upon the four great gifts.

In this world, as a matter of common experience, happiness seems to be connected with outside things, or persons, or "values." To values, most of all. Also, you may not get happiness in any way that you can "swear" you have it. And, as long as you can doubt that you are happy, you probably are not.

In addition, and peculiarly, if you try to "look at" happiness, it tends to disappear.

Now, bring "contentment" into the picture. Compare it to happiness.

Contentment is a little different. You can be "content" even with some unhappiness. When you get that far, you have accomplished a great thing. If you get love, peace, freedom, and security, you get, at least, contentment. And you will be on your way into happiness, too.

Examine, with me, some academic ideas about happiness.

In the Britannica Great Books Yearbook, "The Great Ideas for 1967," the editors introduce an article called, "The Idea of Happiness," by V. J. McGill. Following, is some of what is said about happiness.

"A quick overall view of Aristotle's account of happiness can be gained by considering certain paradoxes about it which he calls to attention. He notes that happiness is something that all men desire, and yet they disagree strongly and widely about what it consists in. Again, happiness involves pleasure, yet it is not identical with pleasure. So too, happiness cannot be attributed with certitude to any man while he lives, even though it is only through the active life that men can become happy. By overcoming and resolving these apparently conflicting statements, one can grasp what Aristotle understands by happiness.

The first of these paradoxes arises from the special and even peculiar relation in which happiness stands to the good. If by 'good' we understand anything desirable, (that is, an object capable of being desired and satisfying a desire) then it is clear that happiness is unique among goods.

Of any good except happiness it makes perfectly good sense to ask why one wants it. It is easy to imagine situations in which a person might ask himself, or be asked by another, why he wants a certain job, or why he wants an education, or wealth, position, fame, or even virtue or knowledge. But it makes no sense to ask this question of happiness, at least as Aristotle understands it. One cannot conceive of making a sentence of the form, 'I want happiness because ... '" (End of quote.)

So we have to be careful in how we approach happiness. We probably need to circle in on it with caution.

You see that you will have to get at happiness by some roundabout way. You gain happiness by ignoring it. Happiness is like a lover who wants you if you seem to pay no attention to him. You will be concentrating on the bait that will <u>trap</u> love, if you do not pay too much attention <u>to</u> love.

Remember, this whole book <u>is</u> about your happiness.

So let's not scare happiness away by talking about it too directly. (Be sure to watch it out of the corner of your eye, though.)

And, as part of this necessarily "sneaky" plan, use the following four ideas, "on trial," to follow it:

1. Some central "power" in the world makes
everything work. (Name that power, or borrow a
word for it.

2. <u>You</u> have an "inside self" that sees and
remembers <u>everything</u>.

3. "Bad" feelings can make you sick.

4. "Good" feelings keep you well.

You want to know how "the power" can be made to work for you, even if you can't tell what that power is. You want to use the powers of the "inside man" wherever you can, to stop wasted effort. And you want to keep your body healthy by stopping the emotions that can make you sick.

In the next section, then, let's examine the idea of "reality."

Section Four
What Is Real?

What about science? How much attention do we pay to science in determining how we define "reality," and what we will or will not accept as being "real."

Generally, you pay attention to science when science is saying yes to something in its own field. You ignore science when it says no to something out of its field. Physical science is in science's field. Spiritual matters are not in science's field.

You know that the things which you believe most come out of what happens to <u>you</u>. You may, on occasion, see a strange accident or some other extremely unusual thing. Maybe you received an unforgettable gift on one of your birthdays, or have won at some very difficult game.

You could easily find it difficult to convince another person of the reality of the strange thing or event that you clearly saw and clearly remember. Some people would be like those who could not believe there was such a creature as a duck-billed platypus, because it was said to have a body and tail like those of a beaver and yet also have a duck's bill and lay eggs. The combination of characteristics seemed to be, to many, just too weird. Yet, the platypus is real. And your own, clearly remembered event is real to you.

Science could not demonstrate the truth or reality of most of our own experiences. You can see how important it is to know that. What happens to you is more real than anything you learn as secondhand knowledge from books, or from the stories of others.

Science could not tell you about the taste of an orange. Or any other taste. I mean, science could not make you "know" the actual taste. No amount of scientific facts would do that. No amount of descriptive writing would do it.

You "know" the taste of an orange -- or any other taste -- by tasting. And, in spite of the fact that you then know what an orange tastes like, you could never make any other person who has not tasted one "know" the taste of it in the same way by telling him about it.

The thing tasted or seen, the smell, sound or "feel" that you experience is more real than any "scientific report." Can science taste anything? Can you taste anything by reading a report about it? Your "tasting" of a taste is more real than any number of statements. The taste is "closer" to you, "part" of you. It is more real than science.

A frequent message of modern science and psychology is that you cannot "trust" your eyes and ears, nose, tongue and fingers. But what do you actually find to be the most real in your life? It is what happens to you every day, what you take in through your senses.

And you put "now" beside "then" to make most of your judgments. You "know" if today's slice of apple pie is better or worse than yesterday's, even if you might not be able to "prove" it.

You will say, "This piece of apple pie is better than the last one I ate." And what you say is not any the less a valid statement because it was not the result of a laboratory experiment. Because it is your own "experience," which is actually the old word for "experiment."

Your own experience is better proof than science. A quote from Sir William Barrett advances a similar thought. "Whatever the humblest men affirm from their own experience is always worth listening to, but what even the cleverest men, in their ignorance, deny, is never worth a moment's notice."

We will, later, look at more about what is real in the world.

But let us consider, again, how much "lab work" we need to do in order to keep track of reality, and whether or not we need to do any at all. Is it possible to affirm meaningful facts without science?

Suppose you have a friend you trust completely. Then suppose he tells you of something that happened to him, perhaps something very bizarre, even incredible. You would not care whether or not science could confirm what he was reporting. If you had to go to a scientist or a laboratory to make up your mind about your friend's story, you would not really be talking to a friend. No. In the case of a good friend, you would tend to accept everything he told you about his own experiences.

So, bearing that in mind, let's go back to your experiences.

Something "inside" of you has the experiences that you find "real." What is it that has the experiences?

You may say, "Me."

What do you mean by "me?" You surely do not mean that "outside person" whom other people see as you. You mean, the "inside" person -- the "real you" -- who sees, hears, smells, tastes, and feels, who thinks and decides.

So, look for your "real" self.

Try this. Close your eyes. Then, "look around" for your "self" in your mind. Now, prepare for a "tricky switch."

That self is not anything that you are looking for. It is, "whoever is doing the looking."

You have found, in this backhanded way, your own "self."

That "self" -- or "whoever is looking" -- is "what things happen to." That self is the most real thing that you know. You can see that it is impossible for anything else to be as close in your experience as that self. That self is more real than anything that you see "outside."

And this means, That the next most real things are those things that "happen" to that self. All "outside things" must "come in" to that self and "happen" to it.

And that is how things "get real."

Things get real through you. You must "make" outside things, and everything else, "real" by "realizing" them. The real must be realized.

The "real" was not made for you by science. You may accept science as an authority in the "laws of matter." But those "laws" are not as real as your own experiences -- not as real as your own "realizations."

Say that you are looking at a tree. A tree does not actually happen to you whenever you see one. Something happens inside of you which you believe a tree caused.

In sleep, you know, you may dream of anything. That "anything" of which you dream, a kind of "thing, itself," is not, somehow, transferred into your mind. That "something" happens inside of you and "appears" to be a thing, itself. And that "something" is inside, not outside, and it is "real."

And that real thing is inside of the "self" that you found when you closed your eyes.

This is important.

Because, to get the four great gifts of love, peace, freedom and security, you must do this: Learn to see what is of that "self," and what is not of that "self."

For instance: The clothes you wear are not part of that self. The roles which you play in everyday life are not part of that self. Even your name is not part of it. If you met someone who had the same name as you do, you would not be able to say that you had met yourself. If another person wore the same sort of clothing as you, that would not make him "you" in any way.

You are one of a kind.

Your "self" is different from any other self anywhere. And if you discover and develop your self's identity, you will increase that difference. You cannot, then, be "common." You cannot become "you" by imitating anyone else. Your self has its own character, strengths, and values. Your self can have a sense of worth that will not change with the changing talk of other people. Your being "yourself" can cause other people to be uncomfortable at times. They like to see you as "common" -- as being just like the "Joes" who try to be like everybody else. But you cannot be common and be free.

Look further at what is "real."

The "taste" of an orange, then, is as real as anything that can happen to you.

Suppose love "happens to you."

Then it is just as real as the taste of an orange.

Suppose peace "happens to you." It is real.

Suppose freedom "happens to you." It is real.

Suppose contentment "happens to you." It is real.

Then consider this:

Science cannot prove the existence of any one of those inner realities. Yet, you can have them all. Science cannot have them. And they are the realest of things.

Because you can experience them in the self, you can have those "goods."

Because you can have them, they can exist.

Take another corner-of-the-eye look at happiness.

Here is a quote from a book used in social work, "The Casework Relationship," by Felix P. Biestek.

"The relationship between a man and a woman, the central theme of songs, novels and dramas, through the ages, is one of the basic sources of human happiness. The difference between a house and a home is not landscaping or interior decorating: ...

"Real happiness is not found in the possession or use of things. A number of things are necessary for living, for the satisfaction of common needs; food, clothing, and shelter are indispensable for subsistance. Things give comfort and satisfaction, but in themselves they do not give happiness. They can only contribute to happiness indirectly."

Who is happy?

One man may have more money than another. Does that mean he is "richer" in the best sense of richness in a "rich" life? Would he necessarily "feel" richer than a man with less money? Would he be happier "because" his house was larger than another's?

Following are some facts about nine very rich men -- very successful men. Did they really need something besides money to be happy?

In 1923, a very important meeting was held at the Edgewater Beach Hotel in Chicago. Attending the meeting were nine of the world's most successful financiers. Those present were:

The president of the largest independent steel company;

The president of the largest utility company;

The president of the largest gas company;

The greatest wheat speculator;

The president of the New York Stock Exchange;

A member of the president's cabinet;

The greatest "bear" in Wall Street;

Head of the world's greatest monopoly;

President of the Bank of International Settlements.

Now, we must certainly admit that here were gathered a group of the world's most successful men. At least, men who had found the secret of making money. Twenty-five years later, let us see where these men are:

The president of the largest independent steel company -- CHARLES SCHWAB -- died a bankrupt and lived on borrowed money for five years before his death.

President of the greatest utility company -- SAMUEL INSUL -- died a fugitive from justice and penniless in a foreign land.

The president of the largest gas company -- HOWARD HOPSON -- is now insane.

Greatest wheat speculator -- ARTHUR CUTTEN -- died abroad, insolvent.

President of the New York Stock Exchange -- RICHARD WHITNEY -- was recently released from Sing Sing penitentiary.

The very well-known member of the president's cabinet -- ROBERT FALL -- was pardoned from prison so that he could die at home.

The greatest "bear" in Wall Street -- JESSE LIVERMORE -- died a suicide.

The head of the greatest monopoly -- IVAR KRUEGER -- died a suicide.

The president of the Bank of International Settlements -- LEON FRASER -- died a suicide.

It would seem that all of these men learned well the art of making money, but not one of them learned how to live. (End of selection.)

Compare the apparent outlook of those nine men with that shown in a remark of the Greek philosopher, Socrates. He was always without money, and did not care for it, or for owning things.

Socrates was passing through the large maketplace in Athens, as you or I might pass through the largest department store in New York City. He looked at all of the goods on sale.

"How many things there are that I do not need," he said.

He probably was a contented man.

Something of Socrates' attitude is implied by another saying, this time, of Jesus. "For what is a man profited, if he gain the whole world, and lose his own soul?"

Did the nine men previously referred to put themselves in exactly that situation?

What are you worth? ... in yourself, without money and property, even without any special, personal qualities?

Read another quote from "The Casework Relationship," by Mr. Biestek. This selection is about human dignity. The words reflect an attitude no different from that in our Bill of Rights. Would the quotation cause you to think more, or less, of yourself, if you accepted it, for the moment, as being true? I did not say, "if you believed it." I merely said, "<u>If</u> it were true, would you be worth more, or less, in your own eyes? Does this quotation say that your value comes out of what other people think of you?

The quote:

"The human person has intrinsic value. He has an innate dignity and worth, basic rights and needs. Man has a unique value in the universe. This intrinsic value ... is not affected by personal success or failure in things physical, economic, social, or anything else. The applicant for financial assistance, the deserted child, the alcoholic lying at the rear door of a tavern on Skid Row, the violent patient in a mental hospital, each has the same dignity and value as the wealthy person, the child of loving parents, the well-integrated person, and even the saint ......

"No individual characteristic forfeits this value. Heredity and environment do not alter a person's basic value. Even unacceptable acts, such as violations of the civil law or of the moral law, do not deprive the person of his fundamental ...... dignity ......

"...... human dignity ...... does not come from personal success ... it does not originate in a Bill of Rights or in a democratic constitution -- these merely proclaim the worth of the individual rather than bestow it ......

"Therefore, because of its origin, the person cannot be deprived of his worth by anything or anyone. Man's worth is inalienable ...... " (End of quote.)

Again, if the statement quoted were true, would you feel worth more, or less, in your own eyes? Would you feel stronger or weaker? Would you accept other people more easily, or not?

What is truth? How is it centered in you? And how does truth relate to the "power?"

What you, personally, see as true is central to everything written so far. I have not tried to give truth to you.

But I am asking you to begin to organize into one piece, all of the things that you think are true in your life. That will be your "complex of truths," the collection of concepts that you accept as truths.

Please, now, relate that complex of truths to the central power you chose a name for; borrowed name, or made up. We need to keep in mind that that power is everywhere. And then we must try to decide the relationship between that power and science.

As before, you are free to call the power (or source) for the world anything that you please.

You might call it simply "the power," or energy, or electricity, light, God, vibration, Uncle Everything, or anything. Just see that "whatever" keeps the universe going is the same everywhere. It is the same inside of you, outside of you, inside the sun, within the earth, anywhere you choose.

Any scientist will tell you that a chair, a steel bridge, a stone -- you, yourself -- are all built of the same kinds of atomic pieces. He sees the world (and the universe) as being the same in basic building-blocks and dynamics everywhere.

The power that you named is in every part of the world. You must try to be lined-up with it in everything you do. Because it is in us and in everything we do. And it affects us all in the same ways. You might say that those consistent ways of affecting us are much like "laws."

Might science affirm these affects to be actual "laws of nature?" Could such supposed laws of nature share any characteristics with "The Golden Rule?"

Ask a scientist for a scientific "law."

He might give you Newton's third law of motion. It is this. "For every action there is an opposite and equal reaction."

Remember how Dr. Hans Selye's studies of stress indicated that "good" and "bad" emotions tend to impel the body toward either wellness or unwellness. The observed interactions between our emotions and our bodies demonstrate that some sort of "laws" govern those interactions.

Can you see that the law called Newton's Third Law of Motion is the same as the "golden rule:" "Do unto others as you would have others do unto you."

The law of equal and opposite reactions is true everywhere: In our world of "sticks and stones;" in the world of our feelings; in the world of our thoughts; and in the world of spirit.

Things that happen to you are the most real part of your life. The law of equal and opposite reaction, or, for us, the Golden Rule, is true in all of the real world. Look more closely for the workings of this law in all that you see in your mind, in all that happens to you.

Then find and stop doing any actions which get returns that you do not want. And then, more importantly, find, and do, actions which get the returns you do want. This is not difficult. But you must want to do it. Because it is the positive actions that finally will ease you into love, peace, freedom and security.

First you will gain contentment. Gradually you will attain the great gifts. Happiness will surely follow. Also with the great gifts comes good health. And real wealth.

On the way, please study your own mind, and feelings, and "the things that happen to you." In all of those, you will see what causes good and bad in your life. Then you will know how to keep out the bad.

Let us review the points to keep in mind; points to test, in order to gain and keep the four gifts of love, peace, freedom, and security. What has been said so far may seem to be difficult to understand or seem unclear. But this is partly because I have not yet said what you will be trying to do about the way you act.

Up to now, I have only tried to get you to "relax" and be "open" as you read. I want your interest; but wish it to be "calm" interest. This is all about you, and for you, remember. Please keep that in mind, as you go over the suggestions which follow.

1. You will wait until the end to decide whether or not any statement that you read is true or false.

2. Decide whether or not you could follow any of the directions, as a test.

3. a. You have chosen a name for the central power that makes everything work.

b. You agree, to test, that your body has an inner "man" or self who senses and records everything in your life.

c. You can be made sick, even unto death, by keeping bad feelings in your mind.

4. a. Your inside self is the most real thing in the world.

b. Because that inner self <u>is</u> the most real of all things, whatever it "knows" is the "next" most real thing. This knowing -- "knowledge" – is more real that anything that you "seem" to see "outside."

c. For the reasons given in a. and b., love, peace, freedom, and security can become more real than anything treated of in science; more real than the "outside" trees, stones, or water.

d. Because your inside, "most real world," has the same "laws" as science, you must use the Golden Rule to be healthy and happy. Failure to obey the Golden Rule causes even worse problems "inside" than outside.

Section Five
Being Practical

What is it to be practical?

See how some of the four great gifts show in "practical" men.

Business is thought of as very practical. A business man is often said to be the "most practical" of men. Perhaps that is because his aim is to "make money." And anything that makes money is thought by most people to be practical. Because, in turn, most people want money, and money is very useful.

One line goes: "If you're so smart, why ain't you rich?" This suggests that the more money you have, the smarter you are. It may be true that it is practical to make money. And "smart" may often equal "rich."

The politician is another person who is thought of as practical.

So is the beggar, who will simply ask you for something.

The salesman, however, may be the clearest example of a "practical" man.

We have, then, the business man, the politician, the beggar, and the salesman.

All four of these men use the same power. They know what "the power" is. They use it to sell you, buy you, save you, or to get something out of you. They try to convince you that they want the best for you.

The salesman will very nearly weep at the thought that you may have to do without his product. The business man works long hours to get his gadget or service to the world to make life easier for all of humanity. The politician will tell you he cares for all of the things that you care for -- that he cares more. He will tell you, besides, that he can do something about it all. The beggar, or "friendly borrower," will call you the nicest, most generous fellow in the world. He will say that he wishes there were more like you. He will tell you that they broke the mold of goodness after they made you. And then follows: "Won't you give me what I want?"

What is it that all of these "practical" men follow?

LOVE.

And all of these people may be sincere in their concern for you. Fortunately, many are.

But look at the code, or "power" that they want to make "work" for them -- that they want to make "practical." See what it is that they all "know" is so practical. See what is the lifeblood of the career of each one.

If they could, each one would like to convince you that he loves you. All such persons do everything they can to make you feel that they love you. You may not believe their concern. You may be suspicious of them. Yet, it is often true that they offer a product or a service that is worth buying. And you sometimes buy.

If these "most practical" men of business and politics and sales and beggary try so hard to use love as a tool, then love IS the most practical thing in the whole world.

Do these practical people have to "mean" it, when it comes to love? Must a man be truly loving to be a good saleman? If so, there would not be many.

But they learn to "wear" the "sheep's clothing of love." They tell themselves that what they sell or purvey is so needed, or so useful, you must have it whether or not you really need or can use it. Everybody knows that a car, a TV, or a water-mattress, is a "necessary item."

Have you ever heard of an atheist preacher? That is, a person who preaches convincingly about God, but who does not believe that God exists. There <u>are</u> such preachers. Such a preacher would be a hypocrite, or a kind of liar, wouldn't he?

But the truth is the truth, even if it comes out of the mouth of a liar. If the gospel is true, it would be true out of the mouth of an atheist preacher, if it is truly spoken. Even the Devil would be an acceptable Bible preacher, if he accurately delivered the text.

But words are not everything. I believe that a man's humanity is found in his feelings -- that when his feeling is one of love or concern for others, he is most human.

Suppose it was just "thinking" that made us human. Then everyone would agree, and say, that being truly human is to care for and to help one another. The fellow who wants something from you doesn't have to be too bright to know he will get it more quickly if he at least pretends to be fond of you. He will soon show you that the word "love" is in his vocabulary. Anyone can use that word, or some word like it, to get something out of you -- your taxes, your apathy, or your good right arm. Christians, communists, and politicians get amazing mileage out of the word love. More mileage than any Japanese motor scooter will get on a gallon of gas.

What most causes people to cooperate with one another?

Three things:

1. Believing that our own interests are best served by working well with others.

2. "Pretended" love.

3. Love, itself.

Most of us have enough brains to know that "being nice" to other people makes it more likely that they will be nice to us. Some of us are too unlucky, or in too much of a hurry, to work with others. Some of us are crazy or in pain. But the rest of us understand point number-one well enough, through experience and observation.

In number-two, I said, "pretended" love. Suppose that you see someone who truly has love, and shows it. You will see certain things in that person. First, that he is at peace, is always sure of himself, and appears to have a steady "power" in his life. If that power is not endless, it still seems to be very great.

Next you will see that the man who acts with love is often successful in getting both respect and property. That is why many people who do not feel anything like love try to look as if they have it. They say, "I don't have to be good to be a success. I simply have to make sure that what I do helps others." Some, who do not care to act loving, but who merely pursue profit, may do good for others in spite of themselves. But the effect of all these behaviors is, more or less, like acting "out of" love. This pattern of acting-out love, even without feeling it, is what I call "pretended love."

Is love all? This is the concern of point number-three.

Love is here considered to be the first of the four great gifts, because it is probable that peace, freedom and security grow out of love, when they are true, or "known." You might feel peace before you see it as love. You may feel freedom or security before you connect either of them to love. You may feel any one of such similar gifts before you discover how it came out of love, or out of some thing or some person that you truly love.

You, yourself, may think of love in any number of ways. You may not believe there is any such thing as love. You may think that you know what love is, but be wrong. Or, you may, in fact, "know" what love is.

If you know what love is, or you think you know, has it given you what it should? Let's see, later.

First we will try to relate love and "the power."

If you think that there is no such thing as love, do something for me. I am asking every reader to do the same.

Take the name you gave to "the power," the "whatever" that makes the universe work. Accept, for now, that that power and love are the same. The power you named, or chose a name for, and love, are one and the same. This is a guess, if you please. You do not have to believe it. Just continue reading with that idea in mind. Also, try to imagine what it would mean if that idea were true.

Now let's go a little further with the idea of love, as we usually think of love.

In spite of the fact that the word love is in everybody's mouth, love is probably very scarce. Most of us spend much of our lives wondering what love is. Many of us never find it. Besides, we can be misled about it. Feelings of appetite, lust, desire, or, even, mere ownership, can be combined to construct a false, faint idea of what love is.

But real love is the link with others. It is somewhat like our feeling of "being," -- our awareness of actually "existing." To have wants like other people, to feel pain, to be hungry, to be pleased, especially to be at peace in love, is to be human. To act the way that those feelings lead us to act is to be <u>humane</u>.

If you are humane, you will not destroy, cause pain, or believe that how you treat someone else should depend upon his appearance, his politics, his race or his country. Negative actions and feelings are sometimes stimulated by factors like the last three, but they should not be.

Being human is to act humanely. Acting humanely is acting lovingly. A psychiatrist, counselor, or preacher would say, "Be human." Accept the advice. Be humane. Imitate the pose of the practical businessman, politician, salesman, the beggar. They love the word love. No word can be so useful, get so much mileage, and not come from a power that is faultily understood. If there is that much smoke, imagine how big the fire must be.

If you and I and the poliltician use the word love, or claim to know how to be human, it may be worthwhile to imagine what it would be like to <u>pretend</u> to be human and loving. We need to try to get through all that smoke to the fire. If we can get there, we may become human and loving, in reality.

I cannot know whether you believe there is such a thing as love. But I have asked you to go along with the notion that the power to which you have given a name and love are one and the same.

Even psychiatrists and psychologists, who claim to be scientific, say that there is such a thing as love. They say that love is <u>not</u> the same as lust, is not a mere "hunger for sex." They say that love is <u>not</u> the same as simple sexual intercourse. They are not very good at explaining what love is, but they are good at saying that love is not just lust or sex.

Let's return to the taste of an orange.

I said earlier that you "know" the taste of an orange if you have tasted an orange. Consider, now, a person who has tasted grapefruits, lemons, and tangerines, but who has never tasted oranges. He might not know the difference between the tastes of those three fruits and oranges. But, on the basis of having tasted the others, he may believe that he can construct a "knowing" of how oranges taste.

He would be wrong. And he would be wrong if he used the same approach to "knowing" love. That is, he could not construct a knowing of love out of experiences of lust and sexual intercourse and orgasms and some sort of "joy of possessing" another person physically.

What is the "taste" of love? Suppose that lust is like grapefruit, sex is like lemons, and pleasant attachment is like tangerines. Many persons <u>do</u> think that what they experience in lust, sex, and pleasant attachment constitutes love, when they have never really "tasted" love. They do not "know" love. They have not "tasted the orange."

The person who eats fruits would be wrong to conclude that the taste of oranges is part of the taste of grapefruits, lemons, and tangerines. He would not "know" the taste of an orange until he had tasted one.

In the same way, the nature and power of love cannot be known to anyone who has not had love "happen" to him. He has got to "taste" love. And when he really "tastes" it, he will find love to be the most powerful, liberating, and enlightening force of all.

Can love be that strong, though? Yes, if it is "true" love. But am I claiming too much for it?

This form of love is very rare. But, again, is it really so strong and so capable of changing a person internally, of transforming one's life?

First, please do believe that this rare love can happen to you. It is not some unattainable mystical rapture. This powerful love causes clear changes in how a person, thinks, talks, and acts. And the changes are for the better. Also, when this love changes you or your friends, you should be able to see it. Conversely, what other people have seen and reported of such love may convince you that it is real, especially if you have seen the same things.

As an example, here is a quote from Emanuel Swedenborg, a Swedish mystic who was born in 1688. Does the love that Swedenborg describes change how the lover looks at things? Could there really be such drastic changes in real life? I do not ask you to accept Swedenborg as an authority, remember. I present his ideas only for you to look at and react to. They are not given as a creed that you must accept. This is offered as a way of seeing love.

Swedenborg has been talking about the kind of love we are trying to see. He calls it "conjugial love." This is the same as "soulmate love." But it is the rare love that changes you and all of your values. You may not think that such love exists. You might, however, agree that lovers commonly behave as Swedenborg says.

Begin quote:

"That at this day love truly conjugial is so rare as to be generally unknown has been stated several times above. That nevertheless it does actually exist has also been shown in its own chapter, and afterward here and there in those that followed. But apart from this, who does not know that there is such a love, which in delightfulness and excellence so transcends all other loves that they all seem of small account? That it surpasses the love of self, the love of the world, yea, the love of life, experiences testify.

"Have there not been, and are there not, those who for the woman desired and solicited as a bride prostrate themselves on their knees, adore her as a goddess, and submit to her as the vilest slaves to her good pleasure? The fact proves that this love exceeds the love of self.

"Have there not been and are there not, those who for the woman chosen and solicited as a bride count wealth, yea, treasures if they possess them as nothing and who lavish them also? A proof that this love exceeds the love of the world.

"Have there not been, and are there not, those who for the woman chosen and solicited as a bride esteem their very life as of no account, and crave death if she does not yield to their petition? A proof that this love is greater than the love of life.

"Have there not been, and are there not, those who for the woman chosen as a bride have been made insane by refusal? May not one rationally conclude from this beginning of that love with many, that from its essence this love dominates over every other love as supreme, and at the same time the soul of the man is in it, and promises to itself eternal beatitudes with her who is his choice and solicitation? Who, wherever he may search, can discover any other cause for this than that he has given up his soul and his heart to the one.

"For if a lover while in that state were given the option to select the most worthy, the most wealthy, and the most beautiful of all the sex from the universe, would he not spurn the option and hold to his chosen one? For his heart is hers alone.

"All this is said so that you may acknowledge that there is a conjugial love of such super-eminence, and that it exists while only one of the sex is loved."

Section Six
Words, Symbols, Meanings And Progress

Would you agree that the behavior of at least some lovers supports the quotation from Swedenborg, at the end of the last chapter?

Ignore the reference to the "soul" in the quotation. Only consider whether or not lovers often behave as Swedenborg said they may.

Let's look at the relationships among words, symbols, and the power. I advised you to ignore the word soul, above, because that word might be part of a language you would not want to accept. But there is a sort of hidden knowledge in some things that we see every day. This knowledge is not deliberately kept from us. It is simply outside of the experience or education of most people. For that reason, we, many times, cannot benefit from signs, words, and shorthand ideas of certain kinds simply because we do not know what is behind them. We will, in passing, examine some ideas which have symbological significance, and try to understand what that significance is.

But, for now, you are still calling the central "power" anything you please. We did ask you to grant, for a time, that love and that central power are the same. So, let us try to see more clearly what the nature of that power may really be.

Most of us, even physicians and those picky psychiatrists, agree that we all search for something like love. You might call it acceptance, appreciation, respect, sympathy, or understanding. We may see it as something else we long for and fear that we may not find. It is easy, then, to believe that everybody is looking for <u>something</u>. You might even agree that many people are looking for acceptance, sympathy, or love, <u>unconsciously</u>, without really knowing what they want.

But each and every searcher knows that he is looking for a "something" that is very valuable: a something that will give life meaning and satisfactions. Often, a person will decide that that something is money, power, fame, or some other enticing material thing.

Let me say, then, that this "something" which everyone wants is love: that only true love can give <u>real</u> value to money, power, fame, or anything else. And we have said that this kind of love is very rare in its strongest form -- so rare that many people do not believe it exists. In that case, the search is often given up.

But this power does exist. And it is the same thing as the central power that you chose your own name for.

Also earlier, and this is very important, (remembering how Will Durant, in his History of Civilization, stated that our sensations are more directly known than the "presumed" objects which "apparently" stimulate our senses) I proposed to you that your inner self is the most real thing in the world. At least it is the most real thing in the world of your own life. You should be able to see that there is nothing closer to you.

When the four gifts of love, peace, freedom, and security become experiences of that most real inner self, they take on the same, greatest, reality.

Which means that whatever it is that causes your experiences is one step <u>less</u> real than your self.

Please continue to go along with those ideas for a time.

And please add the following:

It is our <u>feelings</u> of joy or pain which are real -- <u>not</u> any of the things that those feelings seem to come from, or with. And those feelings can be changed, as you have seen in yourself, from good or bad, by how we <u>look</u> at the things that seem to cause the feelings.

So our feelings can be changed greatly by our "point of view." And, again very importantly, we can construct a point of view to fit our own likes, dislikes and beliefs, by refusing to accept without question the everyday opinions of most people about everything.

And you do not, in remolding points of view, change any law of science. You merely look at the world from a new position.

You see, in this, that love, peace, freedom, and security are real. True, they are not "scientific." But we know that they are real because we feel them. We know this for the same reason that we know a pain is real, or sorrow, or joy: because we feel pain, sorrow, or joy. If our feelings are not scientific, that is science's hard luck, not ours.

Please explore with me the value of the four great gifts relative to other desirable things.

Wealth is clearly less valuable than health. Many persons willingly part with their last dollar to be freed from some sickness. You cannot put a price tag on health.

You have heard Swedenborg describe a kind of love that he called conjugial. He showed you how love can drastically change the value system and behavior of the one who loves.

Listen to another man, a research biologist like Dr. Hans Selye. You will remember that Dr. Selye investigated physical illnesses as they appear to be affected by the mind.

Dr. Alexis Carrell is the biologist to whom we now refer. He was perhaps the best-known laboratory scientist of the early 1900's. He worked at the Rockefeller Institute for Medical Research in New York City. His approach to life was naturally influenced by his work in biology. He believed that he saw in history and in living matter much more than what was material. The following quotation is from his book, "Man the Unknown." Dr. Carrell is discussing what human beings see as "progress," and what some of the desirable or undesirable effects of progess upon us might be.

"Everybody is interested in things that increase wealth and comfort. But no one appears to understand that the structural, functional and mental quality of each individual has to be improved. The health of the intelligence and of the affective sense, moral discipline and spiritual development are just as necessary as the health of the body and the prevention of infectious diseases.

"No advantage is to be gained by merely increasing the number of mechnanical inventions. It would perhaps be as well not to accord so much importance to the discoveries of physics, atronomy and chemistry. In truth pure science never directly brings us any harm. But when its fascinating beauty dominates our minds and enslaves our thoughts in the realm of inanimate matter, it becomes dangerous. Man must now turn his attention to himself, and to the cause of his moral and intellectual disability. What is the good of increasing the comfort, the luxury and beauty, the size and complexity of our civilization, if our weakness prevents us from guiding it to our best advantage? It is really not desirable to go on elaborating a way of living that is bringing about the demoralization and disappearance of the best elements of the great races. It would be far better to pay more attention to ourselves than to construct faster steamers, more comfortable autos, cheaper radios, or telescopes for examining the structure of remote nebulae. What real progress will be accomplished when aircraft take us to Europe or to China in a few hours? Is it necessary to increase production unceasingly simply so that men may consume larger and larger quantities of useless things? There is not a shadow of a doubt that mechanical, physical and chemical sciences are incapable of giving us intelligence and moral discipline, health, nervous equilibrium, and peace."

Here is Dr. Carrell again. He asserts that the body can be changed by the way we look at things, and by our emotions.

" ..... envy, hate, fear, when these sentiments are habitual, are capable of starting organic changes and genuine diseases. ..... Thought can generate organic lesions. The instability of modern life, the endless agitation, and the lack of security create states of mind which bring about nervous and organic disorders of the stomach and intestines, defective nutrition, the passage of intestinal microbes into the blood. Colitis and the accompanying infections of the kidneys and bladder are the remote results of mental and moral imbalance. Such diseases are almost unknown in social groups where life is simpler, and not so agitated, where anxiety is less constant. ....."

"In all countries and at all times, people have believed in miracles, in the more or less rapid healing of the sick at places of pilgrimage, at certain sanctuaries. But after the great growth of science during the 1800's such belief completely disappeared. It was generally said, not only that miracles did not exist, but that they could not exist. As the laws of thermodynamics make perpetual motion impossible, physiological laws oppose miracles. Such is still the attitude of most physiologists and physicians.

"However, in view of the facts observed during the last fifty years, this attitude cannot be sustained.The most important cases of miraculous healing have been recorded by the Medical Bureau at Lourdes. Our present conception of the influence of prayer upon pathological lesions is based upon the observation of patients who have been cured almost instantaneously of various ailments, such as peritoneal tuberculosis, cold abscesses, osteitis, suppurating wounds, lupus, cancer, and so forth.

"The course of healing changes little from one person to another. Often, an acute pain. Then a sudden sensation of being cured. In a few seconds, or a few minutes, at most a few hours, wounds are cicatrized, pathological symptoms disappear, appetite returns.

"Sometimes functional disorders vanish before the anatomical lesions are repaired. The skeletal deformations of Pott's disease, the cancerous glands, may still persist two or three days after the healing of the main lesions. The miracle is chiefly characterized by an extreme acceleration of the process of organic repair. There is no doubt that the rate of cicatrization of the anatomical defects is much greater than the normal one. The only condition indispensable to the occurence of these phenomena is prayer. But there is no need for the patient himself to pray, or even to have religious faith. It is enough that someone near him be in a state of prayer. Such facts are of profound significance. They show the reality of certain relations of still unknown nature, between psychological and organic processes. They prove the objective importance of spiritual activities, which hygienists, physicians, educators, and sociologists have perpetually neglected to study. They open to man a new world."

I remind you again that I am not telling you to accept any authority, or to assent to anything, so far, as being true. Just keep in mind yet the power that you have given a name to. And please continue to read with an open mind.

That "power," incidentally, is being seen, felt and talked about by all of the people we quote. Try to <u>look under</u> all the different ways they talk. The mystic, the scientist, the social worker, the physician, the biologist, the philosopher, and the preacher all <u>feel</u> "something" that they believe is real. Try to see or feel that reality if you can. Try to begin to get its "mood" or "feel." Try to begin to sense how it works, even if you and I might not agree about <u>what</u> it is.

In our study, it does no harm to at least "pretend" to be a little ignorant. Because you do not need to know what the power is. You only need to learn how to use it. To suppose that you need to know what the power is in order to use it, is like saying that you need to know how to build an automobile before you can drive it.

If your car works, and is kept in repair, all that you need to know to get downtown is how to turn the starter key and to steer the car. If you had to be a mechanic, and to know how to make and repair the car, you would never get out of the driveway.

You see, I am not trying to show you any "brand" of car, or any "brand" of creed or code that you must use. I want to help you get and keep the "feel" of the "way" that the power, as <u>you</u> understand it, can be used in <u>your</u> life.

Section Seven

Open Secrets
And The Conversion Experience

Now, about "open secrets."

Open secrets are statements that everybody knows, but that almost nobody understands.

An interesting fact about open secrets is this: The reason that nobody understands them is exactly because everybody can, and does, say them.

Wise men, including mystics, know that the best way to hide their secrets is to tell them to everyone.

This works because every open secret needs a key. Most people will not know that key. They would probably not recognize it even if they had a "dictionary definition" of the key. But, mostly, they cannot use the key because they do not "feel" how to use it.

An example of "open-secret hiding" -- "hiding by not hiding" -- is shown in Edgar Allen Poe's story, "The Purloined letter."

A letter was missing, supposedly stolen. Everyone was looking in every hiding-place he could think of to find it, but were having no luck.

The reason was, the letter was out in the open. It was in clear sight, in a letter holder. No one expected the letter to be there. Everyone was caught up in the idea that it had to be carefully hidden.

Open secrets are like that letter. They are common. They can be seen or heard at any time. They can be understood in many ways. But most of us do not get beyond the "everyday," or "logical," way of understanding.

Here is one such saying.

"The power of love -- not the love of power -- can bring peace."

The saying can be looked at from multiple levels of meaning. One level of guidance in that statement could apply to countries and states, political parties and individual politicians. At another level, the saying could guide the behavior of families toward one another, or among people in a family -- everybody.

But now we come to the most important level of use for the stated rule.

Inside of ourselves. Within each of us, is where we should use the open secrets in the saying: "The power of love -- not the love of power -- can bring peace."

And what is the "key" to that phrase?

Love.

But, love, in what sense?

You can see that you might get by for some time with a logical, educated, or "smart" understanding of love. You probably also see that "knowing" or "feeling" love would make it much easier to use the power in the quote.

So, is love in us? If love is within us it enables us not only to know how to use the power in the phrase above, but to use the power in many other phrases as well.

The last quotation, and all others, so far, are different ways that the minds of human beings "feel" the power in life. People may use different words, but they are all looking at and reacting to the same power. So are you. You react to the same power all the time. Try to identify that power in everything you do, every day.

The next quotation is from George Bernard Shaw, the English playwright. It is one of his representations of love.

I had always thought of Shaw as a worldly man, an agnostic. Perhaps he was an agnostic. But see how insightfully he describes love. These are statements that he has a man make in a play called "A Village Wooing." The conversation is between a man, referred to as "A," and a woman, referred to as "Z." The man is a poet, and not very practical. The woman has just got him to ask her to marry him. The man has bought the store in which the woman is now the clerk.

The man, "A," begins.

A. Well, you already have me -- as an employer. And you are independent of me, and can leave me if you are not satisfied.

Z. How can I be satisfied when I can't lay my hands on you? I work for you like a slave for a month on end; and I would work harder as your wife than I do now; but there are times I want to get hold of you in my arms -- every bit of you; and when I do I'll give you something better to think about than the starry heavens, as you call them. You'll find that you have senses to gratify as well as fine things to say.

A. Senses! You don't know what you're saying. Look about you. Here in my shop I have everything that can gratify the senses; apples, onions, and acid drops; pepper, mustard; cosy comforters, hot-water bottles. Through the window I entertain my eyes with the old church and market place, built in the days when beauty came naturally from the hands of medieval craftsmen. My ears are filled with delightful sounds, from the cooing of doves and humming of bees to the wireless echoes of Beethoven and Elgar. My nose can gloat over our sack of fresh lavender or our sixpenny Eau de Cologne when the smell of rain on the dry earth is denied me. My senses are saturated with satisfactions of all sorts. But when I am full up to the neck with onions and acid drops; when I am so fed up with medieval architecture that I had rather die than look at another cathedral; when all I want is rest from sensation, not more of it, what use will my senses be if the starry heavens still seem no more than a senseless avalanche of lumps of stone and wisps of gas ... if the destiny of man holds no higher hope to him than the final annihilation of so mischievous and miserable a creature.

Z. We don't bother about all that in the village.

A. Yes you do. Our best seller is Old Moore's Almanack; and after it comes Napoleon's Book of Fate. Old Mrs. Ward would never have sold the shop to me if she had not become persuaded that the Day of Judgment is fixed for the seventh of August next.

Z. I don't believe such nonsense. What's it got to do with you and me?

A. You are inexperienced. You don't know. You are the dupe of words like sensuality, sensuousness, and all the rest of the twaddle of the Materialists. I am not a materialist: I am a poet; and I know that to be in your arms will not gratify my senses at all. As a matter of mere physical sensation you will find the bodily contacts to which you are looking forward neither convenient nor decorous.

Z. Oh, don't talk about it like that. You mustn't let yourself think about it like that.

A. You must always let yourself think about everything. And you must think about everything as it is, not simply as it is talked about. Your second-handed gabble about gratifying my senses is only your virgin innocence. We shall get quite away from the world of sense. We shall light up for each other a lamp in the holy of holies in the temple of life; and the lamp will make the veil transparent. Aimless bits of stone blundering through space will become stars in their spheres. Our dull purposeless village existence will become one irresistible purpose and nothing else. An extraordinary delight and intense love will seize us. It will last hardly longer than the lightning flash which turns the black night into infinite radiance. It will be dark again before you can clear the light out of your eyes -- but you will have seen -- and for ever after you will think about what you have seen, and not gabble catchwords invented by wasted virgins that walk in darkness. It is to give ourselves this magic moment that we will hold each other in our arms -- and the world of senses will vanish. Then for us there will be nothing ridiculous, nothing uncomfortable or unclean, nothing but pure paradise.

Z. Well, I am glad you take a nice view of it; for, now I come to think of it, I never could bear to be nothing more to a man than a lollipop. But you must not expect too much.

A. I shall expect more than you ever dreamt of giving, in spite of the endless audacity of women. What great men would ever have been married if the female nobodies who snapped them up had known the enormity of their own presumption? I believe they all thought they were going to refine, to educate, to make real gentlemen of their husbands. What do you intend to make of me, I wonder?

Z. Well, I have made a decent shopkeeper of you already haven't I? But you needn't be afraid of my not appreciating you. I want a fancy sort of husband, not a common villager that any woman could pick up. Why, I shall be proud of you. And now I've nailed you, I wonder at my own nerve.

A. So do I.

Z. I'm not a bit like that, you know, really. Something above and beyond drove me on. I can't make a fine speech about it, like you -- but it will be all right. I promise you that.

End of the extract from "A Village Wooing."

"A" spoke of a very great change in one's view of the universe. He described how the non-physical "knowing" of love changes the meaning of the whole outside-world for us forever.

How about you?

Do you love any one thing in the world so much that you would give up everything else for it? Should you love anything that much? Perhaps to love a person is better.

Some people, when they have touched the power, love it. Some of them then think that the power is God. That sort of contact with the power may be the best. But to truly love another person is as far as most of us get.

Two quotations from a book of Irish fairy tales are given below. Both quotations say how a woman is loved.

First:

" ... Mongan loved Duv Laca of the white hand better than he loved his life, better than he loved his honour. The kingdoms of the world did not weigh with him beside the string of her shoe. He would not look at a sunset if he could see her. He would not listen to a harp if he could hear her speak, for she was the delight of the ages, the gem of time, and the wonder of the world till doom."

Second:

" ... Indeed, Fionn loved Saeve as he had not loved a woman before and he would never love again. He loved her as he had never loved anything before. He could not bear to be away from her. When he saw her he did not see the world, and when he saw the world without her it was as if he saw nothing, or as if he looked upon a prospect that was bleak and depressing. The belling of a stag had once been music to Fionn, but when Saeve spoke that was sound enough to him. He had loved to hear the cuckoo calling in the spring from the tree that is highest in the hedge, or the blackbird's jolly whistle in an autumn bush, or the thin sweet enchantment that comes to mind when a lark thrills out of sight in the air and the hushed fields listen to the song. But his wife's voice was sweeter to Fionn than the singing of a lark. She filled him with wonder and surmise. There was magic in the tips of her fingers. Her thin palm ravished him. Her slender foot set his heart beating; and whatever way her head moved, there came a new shape of beauty to her face.

"'She is always new,' said Fionn. 'She is always better than any other woman -- she is always better than herself.'

"He attended no more to the Fianna. He ceased to hunt. He did not listen to the songs of the poets or the curious sayings of the magicians ... for all of these things were in his wife ... and something that was beyond these was in her also.

"'She is this world and the next one; she is completion,' said Fionn." (End of Irish fairy-tale quotes.)

Imagine such a love. Do you love anyone as much as is said in those two quotes? Do you believe anyone <u>does</u> love that much? Do you suppose that <u>you</u> could love anyone that much?

Please do this. Try to <u>begin to imagine</u> what it would be like to love with such intensity. Can you make a mind-picture of how loving that much should cause you to behave?

So, imagine that you love someone that much. Now, (very important) see the person that you love so much as being part of <u>everything else in the world</u>. Then the way you want to treat that person whom you love, is the way you should want to treat the whole world.

As a reminder, I hope that you are trying to "feel" or "sense" the power "under" all of these words. And I trust that you did name the power to suit yourself, and are using that name as a "test" name. Whatever you do, that power is what we are trying to meaningfully "move over." I am not teaching you literature. And I do not want to irritate you by having you read things that you might not want to. Simply try to get the "feel" of what is happening under it all. My only aim is to facilitate that process.

Now come materials that have to do with a kind of "lighting-up" of the mind. Following are two extracts from a book titled "Cosmic Consciousness," by Doctor Richard Bucke. He tells of people who believed they had been "let in on" knowing "the power."

The first extract is about the doctor himself. A friend of his describes what started Doctor Bucke investigating the kinds of events dealt with in his book.

First:

" ... It was early spring at the beginning of his thirty-sixth year. He and two friends had spent the evening reading Wordsworth, Shelley, Keats, Browning, and especially Whitman.

"They parted at midnight and he had a long drive in a hansom cab in an English city. His mind was deeply calm with quiet enjoyment from the reading and talk of the evening.

"All at once, without any warning, he found himself wrapped around as it were by a flame-coloured cloud. For an instant he thought the city was on fire. Then he saw that the light was in himself. Right afterward he was flooded with heavenly joy and boundless power to think. He said that no words could picture the exquisite gladness and grandeur of it.

"Into his brain streamed one lightning flash of divine splendor. This divine splendor filled his life with light during all his years thereafter. Upon his heart had fallen one drop of divine bliss, leaving an after-taste of heaven which he never lost.

"He did not just believe; he saw and knew that the universe is not dead matter but a living Presence. He saw and knew that the soul of man is immortal. He saw and knew that the universe is so built and ordered that all things work together for the good of each and all. He saw and knew that the foundation of the world is what we call love, and that the happiness of everyone is in the long run absolutely certain.

"Dr. Bucke claimed that he learned more within the few seconds during which the light lasted than in the previous months or even years of study, and that he learned much that no study could ever have taught.

"The light itself lasted only a few seconds but its picture lasted throughout his life. It was impossible for him ever to forget what he saw and knew in those golden moments of divine splendor. Neither could he ever doubt the truth of what was shown him. There was no return of the experience that night or at any other time."

Begin the second quote from "Cosmic Consciousness," from the poet Walt Whitman.

"I will describe as well as I can the supreme event of my life which undoubtedly is related to all else and is the outcome of years of passionate research.

"I had come to see that my need was greater, even, than I had thought. The pain and tightness deep in the core and center of my being were so great that I felt as might some creature which had outgrown its shell and yet could not escape.

"What it was I knew not except that it was a great yearning -- for freedom, for larger life -- for deeper love. There seemed to be no response in nature to that infinite need. The great tide swept on uncaring, pitiless, and, strength gone, every earthly hope wiped out, nothing was left to me except to give all of myself up to God.

"So I said: 'There must be a reason for it, a purpose in it, even if I cannot grasp it. The power in whose hands I am may do with me AS IT WILL! It was several days after this decision before the point of complete surrender was reached. Meantime, with every sense inside me I searched for that power, whatever it was, which would hold me when I let go.

"At last, I met with a strange growing strength in my weakness, as I LET GO OF MYSELF! In a short time, to my surprise, I began to feel a sense of physical comfort, of rest, as if some strain of tightness was removed. Never had I experienced such a feeling of perfect health. I wondered at it. And how bright and beautiful the day!

"I looked at the sky, the hills and the river, amazed that I had never realized how divinely beautiful the world was. The sense of lightness and growing bigness kept increasing, the wrinkles smoothed out of everything, and there was nothing in the world that seemed out of place.

"At dinner I remarked, 'How strangely happy I am today!' If I had realized then, as afterward, what a great thing was happening to me, I should have doubtless quit my work and given myself up to the thought of it, but it seemed so simple and natural (with all the wonder of it) that I and my affairs went on as usual.

"The light and color glowed, the atmosphere seemed to quiver and vibrate around and in me. Perfect rest and peace and joy were everywhere, and stranger than all, there came to me a sense of some serene, magnetic presence -- grand and engulfing.

"The light and joy within me were becoming so intense that by evening I became restless and wandered about the rooms, scarcely knowing what to do with myself. Retiring early that I might be alone, soon all the world as we know it was shut out. I was seeing and understanding the sublime meaning of things, the reasons for all that had before been hidden and dark.

"The vast truth that life is a spiritual unfolding, that this life is but one step in the blooming of the soul, burst upon my dazzled vision with overwhelming grandeur. Oh, I thought, if this is what it means, if this is the outcome, then pain is sublime! Welcome, centuries of suffering, if it brings us to this!

"And still the splendor increased. Presently what seemed to be a swift oncoming tidal wave of splendor and glory came down upon me and I felt myself being surrounded, swallowed up.

"I felt myself going -- losing, myself. Then I was terrified, but with a sweet terror. I was losing consciousness, my identity -- but was powerless to hold myself. Now came a period of rapture so intense that the universe stood still as if amazed at the unutterable majesty of the spectacle!

"Only one in the entire infinite universe! The All-loving, the Perfect One! The perfect Wisdom, Truth, Love, Purity! And with the rapture came the insight. In that same wonderful moment of what might be called divine bliss came the light.

"I saw with vivid inner vision the atoms or molecules, of which seemingly the universe is made -- I know not whether material or spiritual -- rearranging themselves, as the universe in its evermoving, everlasting life passed from order to order.

"What joy when I saw that there was no break in the chain -- not a link left out -- everything in its own place and time. Worlds, systems, all blended into one harmonious whole. Universal life, alike with universal love!

"How long that period of intense rapture lasted I do not know -- it seemed an eternity -- it might have been only moments. Then came relaxation, the happy tears, the murmured, rapturous feeling. I was safe; I was on the great highway, the upward road which humanity had trod with bleeding feet but with deathless hope in the heart and songs of love and trust on the lips.

"Now I understood the old eternal truths, yet fresh and new and sweet as the dawn. How long the vision lasted I cannot tell. In the morning I awoke with a mild headache, but with the spiritual sense so strong that what we call the actual, material things surrounding me seemed shadowy and unreal.

"My point of view was entirely changed. Old things had passed away and all had become new. The ideal had become real, the old REAL had lost its former reality and become shadowy. This shadowy unreality of worldly things did not last many days.

"Every longing of the human heart was satisfied, every question answered, the 'pent-up, aching rivers' had reached the ocean -- I loved infinitely and was infinitely loved! The universal tide flowed in upon me in waves of joy and gladness, pouring down over me as in torrents of fragrant balm.

"This describes actual sensation. The infinite love and tenderness seemed to really stream down over me like holy oil healing all my hurts and bruises. How foolish, how childish, now seem bad temper and discontent in the presence of that divine majesty.

"I had learned the grand lesson that suffering is the price which must be paid for all that is worth having -- that in some mysterious way we are refined and sensitized, doubtless largely by it, so that we are made open to nature's higher, finer sway. This, if true of one, is true of all.

"And feeling and knowing this, I do not rave as I once did, but am 'silent as I sit and look out upon all the sorrow of the world' -- 'upon all the meanness and agony without end.' That sweet eternal smile on nature's face! There is nothing in the universe to compare with it -- such a joyous repose and sweet unconcern -- saying to us, with tenderest love: All is well, always has been and always will be.

"To me the divine light is magnetic or electric; a force is liberated in the brain and nervous system; an explosion takes place. The fire that burned in the breast is now a mounting flame. Several times, weeks after the light described, I distinctly felt electric sparks shoot from my eyes.

"I looked forward with somewhat of a dread to the summer and when it came its light and its wealth of color, although delightful, were almost more than I could bear. We think we see, but we are really blind. IF we could SEE!

"One day for a moment my eyes were opened. It was a morning in early summer. I went out in happy, peaceful mood to look at the flowers, putting my face down into the sweet peas, enjoying their fragrance, seeing how bright and separate were their form and color.

"The pleasure I felt deepened into rapture; I was thrilled through and through, and was just beginning to wonder at it when deep within me a veil or curtain parted -- and I became aware that the flowers were alive and could think!

"They were in commotion! And I knew that they were throwing off electric sparks! What an unveiling it was! The feeling that came to me with the vision is indescribable -- and I turned and went into the house with unspeakable awe.

"In experience, the divine light was not something <u>SEEN</u> -- a sensation as distinct from an emotion -- it was emotion itself, ECSTASY. It was the gladness and rapture of love, so intense that it became an ocean of living, palpitating light -- a brightness brighter than the sun -- its warmth and tenderness filling the universe. That infinite ocean was eternal love, the soul of nature, and all one endless smile!

"What astonished me beyond all was, as the months went on from that September, a deepening sense of a Holy Presence. There was a hush on everything, as if nature were holding her breath in adoration.

"At times the feeling came over me with such force as to become heavy, almost painful. It would not have surprised me if the very rocks and hills had burst forth in one great anthem of praise. There were times I felt as if they MUST, to relieve my feelings.

"The rent veil, the holy of holies, cherubim with folded wings, tabernacles, temples -- I saw that they were symbols; attempts of men to picture an inner experience. Nature touched me too closely. Sometimes I felt weighed down by it, such intense uplift weakened me and I was glad when I could have a common day.

"There was and is still, though not so strongly as earlier, a very decided and peculiar feeling across the brow above the eyes as of tightness gone, a feeling of more room. That is the physical sensation. The mental is a sense of majesty, of serenity, which is more noticeable when out of doors.

"Another very decided and peculiar effect followed the picture above described; that of being a center. It was as if surrounding and touching me on all sides were the softest, downiest pillows. Lean in what direction I might, they were there.

"A pillow or pillows which fitted every tired spot so that, though I was distinctly sensitive to their lightest touch, there was not the slightest hindrance to movement, and yet the support was as lasting and solid as the universe. It was 'the everlasting arms.' I was anchored at last. But to what? To something inside myself?

"The feeling of completeness and everlastingness in myself is one with the completeness and everlastingness of nature. The sensation is quite different from any that I had before the light, and has sprung from that.

"I often wonder what has happened; what change has taken place in me to so balance me and make me stand out by myself. My feeling is as if I were separate from all other beings and things, as is the moon in space, and at the same time I feel one with nature.

"Out of this event was born a neverfailing trust. Deep in the soul, below pain, beneath all the raging storm of life, is silence vast and grand: an infinite ocean of calm which nothing can disturb; Nature's own exceeding peace which 'passes understanding.'

"That which we longingly seek, here and there, upward and outward, we find at last WITHIN OURSELVES. The kingdom within! The indwelling God! -- are words whose sublime meaning we never shall understand." (End of Walt Whitman quote.)

I do not say you could, or should, have an experience just like that of either Dr. Bucke or Walt Whitman. Perhaps you could have. I don't know if you should. I don't know how or why these dramatic openings of awareness occur.

I do say that you can get all the good of an experience like theirs by looking closer at some things you see every day. You can get love, peace, freedom and security by using your mind and your will-power. You do not have to wait for a personal, dramatic "flash of light." You will see more, here, about using mind and will-power later. For now, continue to try to "feel" what is the same in all that you read about what gives the power.

Look at another example of a "flash of light" like the last two, this time, from the Bible. The event is not described as fully as those previous. But you can tell that it involves much the same kind of "inside thing," and that it changed the meaning of the "outside."

This is Saul, who, because of this experience, became the apostle Paul. The text is Acts, Chapter 9. Remember, Saul was quite rich and respected. He was a lawyer and was in the highest legal body of the Jews, the Sanhedrin. He had been "hunting down" Christians until this time. Not long before this incident, he had held coats for members of a Jewish mob which stoned to death Stephen the martyr.

Saul is traveling to Damascus from Jerusalem. With him he has papers giving him the right to arrest any Christians and take them back to Jerusalem for trial.

Begin quote:

"Saul, yet breathing out threatenings and slaughter against the disciples of the Lord, went unto the high priest,

2 And desired of him letters to Damascus to the synagogues that if he found any of this way, whether they were men or women, he might bring them bound back to Jerusalem.

3 And as he journeyed, he came near Damascus; and suddenly there shined round about him a light from heaven:

4. And he fell to the earth, and heard a voice saying unto him, 'Saul, Saul, why persecutest thou me?'

5 And he said, 'Who art thou, Lord?' And the Lord said, 'I am Jesus whom thou persecutest; it is hard for thee to kick against the pricks."

6 And he trembling and astonished said, 'Lord, what wilt thou have me do?' And the Lord said unto him, 'Arise, and go into the city, and it shall be told thee what thou must do.'

7 And the men who journeyed with him stood speechless, hearing a voice but seeing no man.

8 And Saul arose from the earth; and when his eyes were opened he saw no man: but they led him by the hand, and brought him to Damascus.

9 And he was three days without sight, and neither did eat nor drink." (End of quote.)

And so, Paul was "illuminated."

Fourteen years later, Paul, now the apostle, mentions this illumination to the people of the church at Corinth. He speaks in the third person, as if of someone else. But his words reveal more of his "flash of light" impressions during his interrupted trip to Damascus. This is from the Second Book of Corinthians in Chapter 12.

"It is not expedient for me doubtless to glory. I will come to visions and revelations of the Lord.

2 I knew a man in Christ above fourteen years ago, (whether in the body, I cannot tell; or whether out of the body, I cannot tell: God knoweth;) such an one caught up to the third heaven.

3. And I knew such a man, (whether in the body or out of the body, I cannot tell: God knoweth;)

4 How that he was caught up into paradise and heard unspeakable words, which it is not lawful for a man to utter.

5 Of such an one will I glory, yet of myself I will not glory, but in mine infirmities.

6 For though I would desire to glory I shall not be a fool; for I will say the truth: but now I forbear, lest any man should think of me above that which he seeth me to be, or that he heareth of me.

7 And lest I should be exalted o'er measure through the abundance of the revelations, there was given me a thorn in the flesh, the messenger of Satan to buffet me, lest I should be exalted above measure.

8 For this thing I besought the Lord thrice, that it might depart from me.

9 And he said unto me, 'My grace is sufficient for thee: For my strength is made perfect in weakness.'"
(End quote.)

This "trip to the third heaven" infused Paul with the vision and knowledge of love that enabled him to write Chapter 13 of First Corinthians. When we come to that chapter, later, remember, it was his ascension experience that equipped Paul to describe love and loving actions so well.

You saw that, regarding his "illumination," Paul spoke of joy, paradise, heaven, revealed knowledge, words "unspeakable" and "not lawful" to be spoken.

Such an experience does not fade. This is shown in Paul's words near the end of his life. He was in prison, soon to be executed. It is clear that the incident on the road to Damascus changed how he saw the "real." The quote is from Titus I, Chapter 4.

"6 For now I am ready to be offered, and the time of my departure is at hand.

7 I have fought a good fight, I have finished my course, I have kept the faith:

8 From henceforth there is laid up for me a crown of righteousness which the Lord, the righteous judge, shall give me at that day; and not only to me but unto them also that love his appearing." (End quote.)

Everything above shows that Paul was let in on many "open secrets."

Jesus refers to open secrets in verses 21 and 24 of Chapter 10 in Luke. He means all the sorts of things clearly stated in His parables but which most men do not really understand. The first remark is directed toward heaven, the second to His disciples.

"21 I thank thee, O Father, Lord of Heaven and of the earth, that thou hast hid these things from the wise and prudent, and hast revealed them to babes ...

24 For I tell you that many prophets and kings have desired to see those things which ye see and have not seen them; and to hear those things which ye hear and have not heard them." (End quote.)

By now you know that the "key" to "those things" is <u>love</u>.

Section Eight
Man, Magic, Your Treasure, And The Philosophers' Stone

What might a coloring book for materialists be like? It could have the qualities reflected in the following quotation.

"This world is all there is, and there ain't no more. This is man. Color him hopeless. This is his history. Color it meaningless. This is his future. Color it with question marks. This is his soul. Color it permanent black. This is his mind. Color it blank. This is his world. Color it charred."

Having read that, let's you and I take another look at reality.

You believe you have a mind. You think this because you have that mind and use it, and so you accept it as being real. You know, or might agree, that science has no way to work with the mind. Science cannot see, feel, hear, taste or smell mind at all with its machines. Science cannot and does not weigh or measure the mind. Yet you know it is real. You don't care that science cannot handle it. And you do not need the permission of science to accept your mind as real. The situation is the same with many other things which you know are real.

Science does measure electrical forces in the brain. It can weigh the brain. Science would not say that this is the same as measuring or weighing the mind. Science fails here because it is trying to understand a kind of non-material reality that falls outside of its scope. Scientists usually will say that they have no tools to investigate religion, and the situation appears to be the same with regard to the mind.

Now consider realities which we think of as "material." "Real" things generally are seen as having gradations of value. We may want certain real things more than we want other real things. We may work harder to obtain things which for any reason we perceive to be desirable. Money is one such thing for most people.

Reverend Jesse Jackson has said that "Money is America's God." He explains why by adding that "God is your ultimate concern, what you give maximum sacrifice for, what you will die for. God is what you worship." Reverend Jackson thinks that Americans will sacrifice the most for money.

Another such statement is from a sermon delivered in The Church of Christ. "Whatever it is that you work for, that is what you love."

Emanuel Swedenborg, the mystic we mentioned earlier, said that "a man is driven by his loves; whatever are his strongest desires."

What do you work for, sacrifice for? What do you care most about? Do you love it? Could that be your god? Whenever you long for peace, could what you work for, or "give" for, bring that peace to you? Might there be something "magical" in what you care the most about?

What is your idea of magic? Would you even grant that there is anything like magic? Would you care whether or not a process was magic if it got you what you wanted?

We noted that you do not have to be a mechanic to start a car and drive it. You may have needed to be shown how to start and drive the car, but you did not need prior training as a mechanic to do it.

Still, if you did not know about automobiles, much about them would seem like magic to you. This is an example of how a lack of experience or knowledge can cause certain ordinary things to look mysterious.

Is there anything that you know does happen which you would feel was magical if it happened to you? If you really knew the central power, do you think you might do things that looked like magic to others?

How do you "feel" about Doctor Bucke's story of being filled with light? How did you feel about Walt Whitman's account of finding a power that "pillowed away" the rough edges of life? What was your reaction to St. Paul's talk of the "third heaven?"

If such events happened to you, would you feel that you had been exposed to a real power? Or would you fear you were losing your mind? On what basis would you decide whether you felt a real power or were losing your mind? Might it not be worthwhile to study the matter further? Or should we reach a verdict before a trial?

Dr. Alexis Carrell described what he believed to be miraculous cures at Lourdes, France. He believed that the cures really happened. His statements about them were like those of a rather detached scientist reporting events which many of his fellow scientists doubted. And most of them did dismiss his reports.

But did his fellow scientists and his other critics do research of their own before they judged his conclusions? No.

Could you accept that all diseases are affected by interactions of our bodies and minds, as stated by Doctor Hans Selye? that the mind and feelings actually affect our health? Does his opinion that "if we keep our minds cheerful, we are more likely to stay well" seem plausible to you?

A medical doctor, John Schindler, wrote a very good book, "How to Live 365 Days a Year." Part of the book was based upon Doctor Selye's research, but most of it came from Doctor Schindler's observations as a practicing physician. Mainly, his book tells us how to stay healthy without unnecessary medicine.

Is it "magic" to keep your health by staying cheerful? If it were magic, would that stop you from using the method to stay healthy? If the method worked, and you saw that it worked, would you agree it was more important that it worked than that you could explain it?

And does magic have to work quickly?

Suppose someone tried to sell you a lamp that was said to be magical, like Aladdin's. The claim is that you can get anything you want simply by rubbing the lamp and asking. Probably, you would kick the salesman out.

If you do not dismiss the salesman, you might want to test the lamp before you buy. If you rub it and get your wish at once, you would probably decide it really was a magic lamp, and buy it.

Again, suppose that the salesman shows you a lamp and says it is magical. You rub the lamp. Nothing happens. You say that the lamp is no good.

The salesman insists that it is. He tells you that it could be weeks, months, a year -- maybe more -- before you see your wish come true. You probably still would not buy the lamp. If so, you could not test it. You would never know whether or not it could make your dreams real.

I do not know if there is such a lamp.

But I do know, and so do you, of many things that do not pay off for a long time.

If you put money in a bank to earn interest, you know that the process will take time. You do not fight with the teller and demand the interest on the same day that you put in your money. But you do expect the interest to grow daily. You know there are rules for the bank.

Look at anything you begin to learn, like swimming, golfing, or skiing. You know that mastering any one of those skills requires certain rules to be followed, and practice. The rules may be easy. The practice is what takes the work, the attention, the "sticking to it" -- even if you know all of the rules from the very first.

There is power or "magic" in many places where we do not see it. We look only at the outside of things. We are not "nosy" enough. We do not dig deep enough.

The following is an example of something that most of us see from the outside only. It is the story of Christ driving the money changers out of the temple at Jerusalem. Forget why he did it. These verses are from St. John, Chapter 2.

"13 And the Jews' passover was at hand, and Jesus went up into Jerusalem,

14 And found in the temple those that sold oxen and sheep and doves, and the changers of money sitting:

15 And when he had made a scourge of small cords, he drove them all out of the temple, and the sheep and the oxen; and poured out the changers' money and overthrew the tables:

16 And he said to them that sold doves, Take these things hence; and make not my father's house an house of merchandise.

17 And his disciples remembered that it was written, The zeal of thine house hath eaten me up.

18 Then replied the Jews and said to him, What sign shewest thou among us, seeing that thou doest these things?

19 Jesus answered the Jews and said unto them, Destroy this temple, and in three days I will raise it up.

20 Then said the Jews, Forty and six years was this temple in building, and wilt thou rear it up in three days?

21 But he spake of the temple of his body."

Where is the main "open secret" in this story? For, open secrets exist at varying levels.

No doubt you know that this is much more than just a chasing of the money changers by Jesus.

The first open secret is that in the last verse: "But he spake of the temple of his body." Jesus's body and the temple are alike.

But the most important open secret of the story is not <u>in</u> the story. It is hidden in what you would find if you thought of the "chase" as happening in a human body. Your body, or mine.

The concept of the "chase" as being inside your body is not something "made up" afterward. It was in the story when the story was first set down.

The temple in the story, then, is your own body. The money changers are various kinds of "bad feelings" that you may have. The animals represent diffferent sorts of thoughts that you may think.

This is exactly the story advanced by Dr. Selye and Dr. Schindler. The bad "feelings" need to be driven out of your body, the temple. Then your body, or the living temple, will do what it should do. It will function properly.

The story given above is true on the spiritual level. There are a number of levels in the one simple story of Christ and the money changers. One level involves the actual chasing-out of the money changers by Christ in the real temple at Jerusalem. Another level has to do with physical and emotional health within the living body. The highest spiritual level is shown in Christ's anger that "business" is being done in God's sacred house. Still another meaning is that in your body-temple, you are like Christ. More, that you are, in fact, a "Church."

All of these open secrets are hidden beneath the "outside" story. You do not see them unless you have "the keys." Those are the "Keys of the Kingdom," supposedly given to St. Peter -- and they were -- but they are available to anyone. The "keys" lie in <u>awareness of the unstated themes</u>. This is <u>knowledge</u> of a non-material kind. (And here, especially, <u>Knowledge</u> is <u>power</u>.) Also, might not the engine of that power be <u>love</u>?

Soon, I will tell you the "second" most important thing you will ever learn. You must decide whether or not you will accept it.

This concerns <u>The Philosophers' Stone</u>. I still do not ask you to believe. I just ask for your attention. At the very last, I have pleaded, please judge.

But, in that judging, you will be judging <u>yourself</u>.

This is the Last Judgment, as named in the Bible. Your judgment of this entire message will be a judgment about <u>you</u>. It has to be. Everything here is too personal for the judgment to be otherwise.

I will tell you about the Philosophers' Stone. But permit me to wander a little before I advance to you "the most important statement."

Through the ages, men have looked for a "philosophers' stone." The philosphers' stone is said to have the power to turn base metals, like lead, into gold. It is also supposed to be a means to gain eternal life. Practically, it stands for very great riches, exactly because it could cause any other metal to be gold, and gold is so very precious.

But the philosophers' stone can do something vastly more important.

In the spiritual realm, the philosophers' stone changes evil to good. It can, therefore, cause the "inside man" to become pure, to increase greatly in value. The philosophers' stone produces spiritual "gold." And heaven is a city made of that gold.

Once you used the philosophers' stone, you would, immediately, be rich on earth. And you would be happy in spirit, in this world, and in heaven. You would, in fact, be in "heaven on earth."

In other words, the philosophers' stone would bring the four great gifts: love, peace, freedom, and security, health and wealth, too. In using it, you would have converted all of your bad feelings and acts into good ones. That would give you a means to have good health. Scientists, psychiatrists, medical doctors, and mystics, all say so. Money, property and social status are poor stuff beside the higher goods gained.

I have not forgot that I am leading up to "the second most important statement." As I said, it is a short one.

But be careful. It is one of the two most important things that I want you to remember out of this all. This statement, I want you to remember whether you can believe it or not. Even if you feel it is really not so much, or is part of some kind of con-game. Especially do I want you to remember the statement if you feel you can not yet use this whole book.

Most importantly, I want you to remember the statement because I want you to test it -- to see if it is true. To see if it can be made true in your life.

You will never be the same when you make it true. It will make your life easier and easier, day by day. And you will never exhaust the knowledge in the statement, or fail to be pleased by that knowledge.

Finding the philosophers' stone usually involves a search, but not always. I have suggested ways to search by discussing open secrets. Now I will try to show you the stone. As I said, it can turn the bad into the good. Philosophers, mystics and alchemists have always looked for it. Many of them found it.

The secret of the stone is the greatest open secret of all. It is like the letter "hidden in the open" in the tale of "The Purloined Letter" It has never been out of sight. It is there for all to see. But everyone misses it. You may feel let down when I finally write the statement. You may already know, or have guessed, what it is. But we are talking about the <u>true</u> philosophers' stone -- and it has been the object of the greatest searches that men have ever made or ever will make. Now you have a chance to share in the enlightenment of those who found it, and avoid the wasted efforts of those who did not.

Paradoxically, the philosophers' stone has been on public display, always. It is as though searchers are sent out to bring back a great store of gold that is supposed to be secreted somewhere and cannot find it because it is piled up in plain sight in the town square. The seekers search through forts and palaces, cellars and attics and caves. They are convinced to the point of blindness that what they are looking for has to be hidden.

How often do you find it difficult to talk to a person because he thinks he knows already all about what you are going to say? Or because he starts after an idea of his own, then hears everything the way he wants to? How many times do others mislead themselves by asking you a question then also answering it?

So, please humor me with special attention when I show you the gold in the public square. Do let me set down the statement. It <u>is</u> gold. It is <u>all</u> the things you search for. It is "the pearl of great price." It is "The Holy Grail." It is "the secret of the ages." It is all of the things that people most greatly desire. It is everything to fill your heart and give your life meaning. It is the treasure that, perhaps, you search for without knowing how to recognize it. It is the gift-package in which you find the great gifts.

Now to the statement. I will <u>capitalize</u> it. I say again that <u>I want it to stick in your mind</u>. I want you to remember it for <u>some</u> reason. Any reason. Even if only because you have become convinced that I am stupid, and are curious as to how I got that way.

This, then, is the <u>true</u> philosophers stone revealed.

THE TRUE PHILOSOPHERS' STONE IS <u>LOVE.</u>

Do you see how that might be true?

You saw how the power we traced through the words of various people changed those people. You saw how this power can make a body healthy. You saw how it solved problems that we have in taking the world as it is, and of taking yourself as you are. These are great changes from a torrent of power that is often lost in a "haze of matter."

The precious gifts of love, peace, freedom and security bloom in that underground river of power.

But did the changes about which you have read need candles or incense or a church? They did not. Did I preach a rite, or vows, or "magic" or "a" Religion to you? No. But those changes happened to the people reporting them, and the changes were true. Might they be magical? What does it matter? When you are starving, you eat, do you not? You don't worry about how the food gets to you.

What would you trade for the gifts of love, peace, freedom and security? Below will be the story of "the pearl of great price." What will that story mean to you in terms of the four great gifts, or in terms of anything you might want?

What is your "heaven?" your "pearl of great price?" What is your treasure? If, indeed, "Where your treasure is, there will your heart be also," where is your heart? Can you see, after the revelation that the philosophers' stone is love, how to read the very short parable of Jesus about the pearl of great price? (Matthew, 13:45-46,) or the parable of the man finding a treasure in a field? (Matthew, 13:44.)

Of the pearl of great price:

" ... the kingdom of heaven is like unto a merchant man, seeking goodly pearls:

46 Who, when he had found one pearl of great price, went and sold all that he had, and bought it."

Of the treasure in a field:

"44 Again ... the kingdom of heaven is like unto a treasure hid in a field; the which, when a man hath found, he hideth, and for joy goeth and selleth all that he hath, and buyeth that field."

You say, "All right, I'll test a new way of acting. I'll try a new way of 'looking at things.' I'll begin to 'sift out' what is worth keeping in my life. I will even accept, for trial, that love is the philosophers' stone.

"But it has to work. I could wait six months or a year -- maybe longer -- for my 'interest.' Or for my wish to come true after I rub the lamp. Or wave the philosophers' stone.

"But <u>how</u> do I rub the lamp, or wave the philosophers' stone -- or do 'whatever?' How must I act? What are the rules? Point me in the right direction.

"Then, tell me <u>what will happen</u>, or <u>what to look for</u>. Do more, if you can. Tell me <u>why</u> I should act in the ways that you will recommend. Don't tell me that I should be good. Tell me why I should follow the rules. Don't tell me to do right because it <u>is</u> right. And don't tell me I may go to hell if I don't do what you say, or that I will end up without friends, or something else like that."

And I, having heard your speech, can only hope to give you enough that is useful.

Luckily, the rules are not difficult to present.

And, remember, I am not calling you to a religion, or a church, or any single creed.

But the rules do contain the power that you wish to use. And that power is whatever <u>you have named it for yourself</u>. That power is <u>under</u> the words. Try to sense or "feel" that power. Do not try to "think" it. Just try to mentally observe whatever goes on within you while you strive to "feel."

That power flows through you all of the time, anyway. You could not live if it did not. That power repairs your body whenever you are ill or injured. It oversees all of the automatic safeguards that are built into you. It builds whatever you need in your body out of the foods that you eat. All of these things are done by the power, and you <u>do not</u> have to think about it.

But you will want to review the rules of that power to learn how to act to "aim" it. You will review the rules for the same reason that the scientist learns the "law of nature." And he learns those laws to know how to "line himself up" with them. He knows that if he wishes to do certain things, he must not go against "the rules."

Notice. The scientist does not obey the rules because he is <u>good</u>, or because he does not want to be <u>bad</u>. He follows the rules because he wants what he does <u>to work</u>.

The rules of acting that you will look at are ways that men of thought through thousands of years have found are "in tune" with "the power." That power is the one that gives us the great gifts of love, peace, freedom and security. Often, it gives health and wealth, too.

The rules do not always tell us "why" we should act in the ways that they advise. But it stands to reason that if you want harmony in your life, you must act from rules that "make the same sense" every day. You may act so "by accident." It is better to act so on purpose.

So what do some particular wise men say? In the next section are four fairly long "sets of rules." Each set of rules comes from a different background. But the "inside message" is the same.

Two other short readings are not so plainly sets of rules. But they probably are. They seem to say briefly what the other four say in greater length.

If you have seen all of these selections before, please read them again in this "personal letter" to you. On review, you may find in them more than you would now believe. They do say <u>how</u> to use the power in open secrets.

Said in another way, the selections tell you how to turn the "starter key" of your "inside car," or "self," even if you are not an "inside self" mechanic.

So, again, please do your best to follow and feel, throughout the Section after this one.

Section Nine
The Rules As Reading Glasses

The rules can be "worn."

The rules may be worn as reading glasses. You put the "glasses" on <u>by reading the rules</u>.

"My Symphony" is a recital of rules by William Henry Channing. The poem describes a way to act "with" the power you are feeling for. This selection uses the common "real world" words that so often fool us with their surface only, but you may be sure that Mr. Channing felt "the power" under all that we see about us.

> To live content with small means;
> To seek elegance rather than luxury,
> and refinement rather than fashion;
> To be worthy, not respectable,
> and wealthy, not rich;
> To study hard, think quietly,
> talk gently, act frankly;
> To listen to stars and birds,
> to babes and sages with open heart;
> To bear all cheerfully, do all bravely,
> await occasions, hurry never;
> In a word, to let the spiritual,
> unbidden and unconscious,
> grow up through the common --
> This is to be my symphony.

In that reading it is easy to see an "outside" way to act. But there is an "inside way of feeling" that goes with the outside way. And we get <u>inside</u> by "looking extra hard" at the <u>outside</u>. Do you see that way to act? Can you imagine how Mr. Channing would have acted if you had met him, understanding that he lived by his code? Would his way of behaving be good for a person? ... for you?

Now, might your neighbor be a gateway to happiness? Might that gateway be shown in this poem by Leigh Hunt?

Abou Ben Adhem

Abou Ben Adhem (may his tribe increase!)
Awoke one night from a dream of peace,
And saw, within the moonlight of his room,
Making it rich, and like a lily bloom,
An angel writing in a book of gold: --
Exceeding peace had made Ben Adhem bold,
And to the presence in the room he said,
"What writest thou?" -- The vision raised its head,
And with a look made all of sweet accord
Answered, "The names of those who love the Lord."
"And is mine one?" said Abou. "Nay, not so,"
Replied the angel. Abou spoke more low,
But cheerfully still; and said, "I pray thee, then,
Write me as one who loves his fellow-men."

The angel wrote, and vanished. The next night
It came again with a great wakening light,
And showed the names whom love of God had blessed,
And, lo, Ben Adhem's led all the rest.

Have you sensed the general state of Abou's feelings -- his character?

From The Bible, from Jesus, St. Matthew 22:36-40.

"37 Thou shalt love the Lord thy God with all thy
heart, and with all thy soul, and with all thy
mind.

"38 This is the first and great commandment.

"39 And the second is like unto it, Thou shalt love thy neighbor as thyself.

"40 On these ... hang all the law and the prophets."

Jesus has said, in so many words, that LOVE IS THE WHOLE OF THE LAW. Verse 39, of course, was the "key" to the reason that the angel put Abou Ben Adhem's name at the top of the list of those blessed by "love of God." Abou loves and is loved by God because he loves his neighbor.

Here is a longer and clearer set of rules.

Desiderata

Go placidly amid the noise and haste and remember what peace there may be in silence. As far as possible without surrender be on good terms with all persons. Speak the truth quietly and clearly; and listen to others, even the dull and ignorant; they too have their story.

Avoid loud and aggressive persons, they are vexing to the spirit. If you compare yourself with others, you may become vain and bitter, for always there will be greater and lesser persons than yourself. Enjoy your achievements as well as your plans.

Keep interested in your own career, however humble; it is a real possession in the changing fortunes of time. Exercise due caution in your business affairs; for the world is full of trickery. But let this not blind you to what virtue there is; many persons strive for high ideals; and everywhere life is full of heroism.

Be yourself. Especially, do not feign affection. Neither be cynical about love; for in the face of all aridity and disenchantment it is perennial as the grass.

Take kindly the counsel of years, gracefully surrendering the things of youth. Cultivate strength of spirit to shield you in sudden misfortune. But do not distress yourself with imaginings. Many fears are born of fatigue and loneliness. Beyond a wholesome discipline, be gentle to yourself.

You are a child of the universe, no less than the trees and the stars; you have a right to be here. And whether or not it is clear to you, no doubt the universe is unfolding as it should.

Therefore be at peace with God, whatever you conceive him to be, and whatever your labors and aspirations, in the noisy confusion of life keep peace with your soul. Thus you will have peace everywhere.

Despite its sham, drudgery and broken dreams, it is still a beautiful world. Be careful. Strive to be happy. (End of "Desiderata.")

The next reading is attributed to Mirza Ahmad Sohrab.

A Persian Rosary

1. Love and serve humanity.

2. Praise every soul -- if you cannot praise him, let him pass out of your life.

3. Dare, dare, and then -- dare more.

4. Do not imitate. Be original. Be inventive. Be yourself -- know yourself. Stand your own ground. Do not lean on the borrowed staff of others.

5, There is no saint without a past. There is no sinner without a future.

6. See God and good in every single face. All the perfections of the Deity are concealed in you. Reveal them. The Saviour also is in you. Let his grace emancipate you.

7. Be cheerful. Be courteous. Be a dynamo of irrepressible happiness. Assist everyone. Let your life be like unto a rose; though silent, it speaks in the language of fragrance. You are a trine of body, mind, and soul. The food of the soul is Divine Love. Therefore, feed your soul on Divine Love -- so that the body and mind be invigorated.

8. Be deaf and dumb concerning the faults of others. Do not listen to gossip. Silence the talebearer with virtuous conversation.

9. Stop the circulation of the venomous germs of religious fanaticism through your veins and arteries and those of your children. Never argue with anyone about his religious beliefs. Religious controversies lead to hatred and separation. Religion is love and fellowship, not theological dogmas and creeds. When you have Love and Sympathy in your heart for your fellowmen, you possess the highest type of religion, no matter by what name you call yourself. Rest assured that the emancipation of the world is through the Nameless God of Love and in the Nameless Religion of Love.

10. Develop the qualities of essential goodness. Every soul is endowed with the attributes of intrinsic beauty. Discover those attributes and hold them before the world.

11. Religion is a personal relationship between man and his maker. For God's sake don't interfere with it, do not organize it, neither try to reduce it to so many statements. Organization, in whatever form, is the death-knell of religion. Do not preach this. Practice and teach it. Let no one dictate to you regarding what you should or should not do or believe in your spiritual life. The final authority is the Authority of the spirit within you and not that of any man, dead or alive. The unerring witness is standing in the center of your being -- all-powerful, mighty and supreme! His is the final testimony. His is the court of last appeal.

12. God's love is in you and for you. Share it with others through association. Do not court separation from creatures but unite with them in love. To know yourself through your fellow men is to know God.

13. Have courage. Realize your divine origin. You are the ray of the Sun of Immortal Bliss. You and the Father are one. The undying radiant Self is in you. Reverence your celestial station. No harm will ever come to you. God's perfect image you are, abiding in the fort of His protection. Association with all people will lead to spiritual unfoldment and not to the deterioration of the soul. Live above the world of faith and infidelity; religion and atheism, orthodoxy and Liberalism; truth and error, angel and devil; and you will be living with and in God ... The God of Absolute Good, the God of Absolute Beauty, the God of Absolute Perfection.

14. In religion there is no compulsion. The path to inner unfoldment is not by restrictions and constraints; not anathema and excommunication, but by constant progress from world to world, from star to star, from constellation to constellation forever and without end.

15. The light of lights is in your heart. Uncover it and let it beam for the illumination of mankind. Do not expect a favor from friend or foe, and you shall never be disappointed.

16. Overcome malice, envy, personal spite and prejudice, and you are the master of destiny.

17. Do not condemn a single soul. In condemning him, you are condemning yourself. Never for an instant forget that he is also a child of God. Upon the great sea of spirit, there is room for every sail. In the limitless sky of truth there is room for every wing.

18. Do not murder the character of a soul under the guise of religion, either by bitter blame or faint praise. Spiritual murder is worse than taking a man's life. Have a sin-covering eye. See only the beautiful and the noble.

19. Be gentle. Be lenient. Forgiving. Be generous. Be
merciful. Be thoughtful. Positive. Soar in the
atmosphere of freedom. Walk in your chosen path
and let no criticism disturb you in the least. This is
the way to success, to happiness, to health, to
prosperity, to glory. Let me walk in it all of my life.
(End Quote.)

You can see how your actions would look if you did live as the Persian
Rosary advises. The words are not important. What is important is <u>why</u> you
should try to live by them. More about the "why" of all this will come in a
later section.

Still trying to "feel," please read the third of the longer sets of rules for
looking at the world. This selection is by the apostle Paul. He, remember,
wrote about going up to the "third heaven." This is Chapter 13 of First
Corinthians. It is probably the most famous of all statements about love, and
it was his vision of heaven in his ascension and of meeting Jesus that enabled
Paul to write it.

"Though I speak with the tongues of men and of the angels, and have not
love, I am become as sounding brass or a tinkling cymbal.

"And though I can prophesy, and understand all mysteries, and am
great in all knowledge, and though I have the gift of faith, and can move
mountains, and have not love, I am nothing.

"And though I give up all my worldly goods to feed the poor, and though
I give my body to be burned, and have not love, it profiteth me nothing.

"Love suffers long, and is kind; love does not envy. Love is not boastful,
and love is not proud.

"Love behaves acceptably. Love does not crave to own anything. Love is
always calm, except for her own sake, then is slow to anger. Love contains
no evil.

"Love turns from wickedness, rejoices in the truth.

"Love bears all things, believes all things, hopes all things, endures all things.

"Love never fails: but prophecies shall fail; tongues shall cease; and knowledge shall vanish away.

"And faith, hope, and love, these three, shall last forever.

"But the greatest of these is love."

Now go to a quotation from the Chinese philosopher Lao Tze. Lao Tze defined a doctrine of "The Way" or "Tao," (pronounced "dow.") That "way" is, ideally, a life path a person may take which keeps him in "harmony" with all things. It may be compared with the "way" of Jesus, where Jesus says "I am the way, the truth, and the life."

Whatever the "way" is, you are already seeing it to some extent for yourself. Whatever the best "way" may be, your own way is a "way," too. But ask yourself this: Is your way getting you what you would like it to? If it is not, then, can your way be "lined up" to get you what you want?

Pretend that you are a wise man who "keeps the 'way,'" while you read what follows.

This statement is more "mystical" than the others. It contains "tricky language." It seems to say that if we want to hit a target, we must aim away from it. Or, if we wish to get to certain things, we must walk away from them. But in "mystical law," this is actually how to get to a goal or to hit the mark. To get "out" we must go "in." To be first, you must be last. To be strong, you must be weak. Note such thoughts below.

"Scholars of the highest class, when they hear about the Tao, earnestly carry it into practice. Scholars of the middle class, when they have heard about it, seem to keep it now and then. Scholars of the lowest class, when they have heard about it, laugh greatly at it.

"The sage puts his own person last, and yet it is found in the foremost place; He treats his own person as if it were foreign to him, and yet that person is preserved. Is it not because he has no private ends that therefore such ends are realized? He is free from self-display, therefore he shines; he is free from self-assertion, therefore distinguished; free from self-boasting and therefore his merit is acknowledged; free from self-complacency, and therefore he acquires superiority.

"It is because the sage is free from striving that therefore no one in the world is able to strive with him. There is no guilt greater than to sanction ambition; no calamity greater than to be discontented with one's lot; no fault greater than the wish to be getting.

"To those who are good (to me) I am good; and to those who are not good (to me) I am also good; and thus (all) get to be good. To those who are sincere (with me) I am sincere; and to those who are not sincere (with me) I am also sincere; and thus (all) get to be sincere.

"He who has within himself abundantly the attributes (of the Tao) is like an infant. Poisonous insects will not sting him, fierce animals will not seize him; birds of prey will not strike him.

"I have three precious things which I prize and hold fast. The first is gentleness; then, economy; the third is shrinking from taking precedence of others. Gentleness is sure to be victorious, even in battle, and firmly to keep its ground. Heaven will save its possessor, by his very gentleness protecting him." (End of quote from Lao Tze.)

You see that these readings do not come out of some "one" religion. No one who was trying to get you into a certain "Church" would use them all.

And I believe you can "feel" that they all call for a way of acting that would look the same in every instance. They do not say how to act at any "one" time. They do not always say "what" to do. But they often <u>do</u> say very clearly what you "must not" do.

However, if your way of looking at things is right by their words, the rules will not cause you to feel any loss of freedom. The rules are positive in life. They first free the "inside man," then the outside man.

So, where is the authority in everything, so far.

The only real "authority" comes out of truth.

Which is very good. Because, fortunately, "the true" tends to work, and, in working, tends to improve your lot and the lot of others. So you can take authority to yourself from the actions that you find will work in your life. If any action gets you what you want, then, in practical terms, it is true because it has got you what you wanted. You may wish to know or understand <u>why</u> it works, and the more you "work it," the more you may discover to prove that it is true.

But each of us, as an individual, labors under a sort of "handicap" in confirming ultimate "truths."

No one of us lives long enough.

For that reason, you must be careful about how you "make" your own truths, which you really must do, at least partly, as you find your way through each day.

Again, we are fortunate, because, with most things that happen every day, "common sense" works all right.

But we have a problem. What we do each day is, in a sense, "tied down" by the way each of us sees the "real world." Also, understanding and evaluating what goes on, and what we have, every day, is made difficult by the fact each of us lives such a, relatively, short time.

A person may live a hundred years. That is just about long enough to develop common sense. But many ideas are "bigger" than every-day ideas. How did the world begin? Was the world made for "some reason?" Is there a God? How did life come to be?

Common sense will not do, for such questions.

Now, no one person lives long enough to find out all the answers, alone. And the answers to such questions have meaning beyond simply satisfying curiosity.

Answering questions like the foregoing also answers other questions: Are you and the world worth anything? or, Are you and the world worth nothing?

Something else complicates answering such questions for most of us: The world, that "world of matter" with which we deal every day gets between us and any concentrated thinking to develop answers.

In everyday life, one may say that we do not "need" to answer those abstract questions. And that is true. It is more exact, however, to say that we do not have the time. We are too "busy." We get a job to take care of food, clothing and shelter. We run into more and more "necessities," in the house, lawn, TV, cars, equipment, and "comfort." At last all of these things take up our entire time and thought, when we are not ill or resting. And this tends to make us feel that only "things," "objects," are real. We grow more and more unsure about, "scared" of, ideas that do not have solid "things" hooked to them. We begin to fear that abstract, "unsolid" ideas are "just dreams" or are "crazy."

And there is another daily complication to thinking beyond material concerns. Everyone around us tends to talk as if whatever "happens next" will most likely be bad instead of good. We joke about how unwisely other people run their lives. In attempting anything new, we often say, "This probably won't go right." We may feel half ashamed if we have shown that we can do something better than anyone else. We must not "show anybody up."

In a lifetime, then, each of us will be "tied up" with "things." Even if we do notice anything out of the ordinary, "strange," we are usually too busy to give it much attention. We will not test the "strange" for its meaning. And so we miss a level of life and truth that we have not seen before.

So what?

So, if you do not know that there is such a thing as a treasure, you will not look for it. Similarly, if you do not believe that there are "hidden laws" in how the world works, you will not try to test them.

Suppose, now, that you have come to believe that there really are "hidden laws." Perhaps because you have learned of the experiences of various persons over thousands of years, and their statements about those experiences have made you curious, maybe even half convinced. You decide to investigate. Because, if the laws that those thinkers define are correct, they should work to get you what you want. And if you really want what they can get you, it makes sense to try them.

And this is where I hope and pray that my approach to "testing the laws" will be of most help to you. I have tried to make my method different from the usual ways of presenting "abstract" ideas or material. I am trying to get through to your "inner self" as directly as possible. And that is why I emphasize "feeling into" or trying to "feel under" the words that I use.

Because love is not gained through "thinking about it." Love must, somehow, "come into you." You must try to set up the conditions to facilitate that entry.

So, hopefully, you are trying, in this process, to get a "feel" for ways of acting that make the hidden laws work. Some rules, creeds, or codes, seem to say in words "how" to act. Your way of <u>looking at</u> the world has a lot to do with getting what you want, because that "outlook" is what actually determines your actions.

You want happiness, at least. And you have seen how happiness seems to be an accident, or by-product, that may go with "other things." I have advanced, for your consideration, the notion that other things which <u>make</u> happiness could be the great gifts of love, peace, freedom and security. We have further surmised that love is perhaps the "source" of the last three gifts just named. For example, you may feel peace or freedom or security -- even something else very pleasant and uplifting -- and that simply would be the way "you" are feeling <u>love</u> at the time.

Now, whether or not happiness come out of love, you have your chosen name for "the power," and that power <u>is</u> where everything comes from. Use the name you like.

But, how can "the power" be detected?

Whenever electricity moves along the wires of a well-made lightbulb, it causes light and heat. The light and heat show that the electricity is there, and that it is active. If the wire or the glass of the bulb is defective, then nothing happens, or wrong things happen. We like to assure that right things happen.

"The power" also moves. It moves through all things, including people. Just as electricity moving in a lightbulb causes the lightbulb to give off light and heat, the power moving through a person causes the person to give off a kind of "light" and "heat."

What does the man or woman give off?

In The Bible, Galatians 5:22-23, we have a picture of what a human being gives off when the power goes through him:

"22 But the fruit of the spirit is love, joy, peace,
long-suffering, gentleness, goodness, faith,

"23 Meekness, temperance: against such there
is no law." (End quote.)

Those two verses seem to show that "a power," referred to as spirit, gives rise to "fruits" of the spirit.

In a person, those fruits would make him patient, temperant, modest, tolerant, in control of himself, not jealous, kind, helpful, loving, at ease, confident; all such things. If you decided that those traits would lead to happiness, you would use them in your way of "taking," or "interacting" with, the world, and you would avoid their opposites. And that approach would make it easier and easier for "the power" to work in you and to produce happiness-making results.

As the power moves more and more easily in a person, it shows more and more clearly in the "fruits" he produces in his daily life. But we must work constantly to keep that positive inner flow from being clouded by "feelings" which do not "go with it." And that involves, again, acting rightly.

Luckily, acting in certain "desirable" ways and <u>not</u> acting in certain other "undesirable" ways is easier than you might think.

You can use a kind of "switch" for your feelings.

But let's review, in the next section, a few other matters before we get to "emotional control."

Section Ten
Ways To See The World

How did "the power" begin? Or, how can it exist?

The materialist says that matter itself is enough to explain anything that we see.

The idealist says that matter, in materialistic terms, is <u>not</u> enough to explain what happens in the world. He believes that there is in or "under" matter a power or spirit which does not need matter. He believes that that spirit adds life, mind, and soul, to matter.

There are three ways in which humans think about "what is true." They may be atheists, agnostics, or be of a religious, or spiritual, persuasion.

The atheist simply says that there is no God.

The agnostic says that he cannot know whether there is a God or not. (The agnostic may be an atheist in practice, since he often assumes for his own purposes that there is no God. He is then an agnostic only outwardly, simply because he has no way to show that God does not exist. He is usually very honest, and may merely argue from a "theory" that there is no God.)

The religious or spiritual person says that there is a God, or a "building" power which created and sustains all things, and that this power has "mind."

The atheist cannot accept that a God "could be" or that God could make the world. He cannot "understand" <u>how</u> God could exist. He asks, as part of a strategy to defend his disbelief, "How could God create Himself," and "How could God exist forever?" And the atheist thinks that either God had to create Himself, or, That God has to exist forever, and the atheist will grant neither choice. The agnostic has the same problem with those two alternatives as does the atheist, and holds the same view of them. The atheist and the agnostic see no sign of God or of spirit.

The weakness of the atheistic and the agnostic way of thinking, is this: Neither the atheist nor the agnostic can "understand" or "prove" how the <u>world</u> can exist, either.

The problem is harder for them about the world. Because the world is "here and is seen." And the atheist and the agnostic must face the same inunderstandable ideas with the world as with God. That is, 1. How could the world make itself? or, 2. How could the world "be" forever? That the world created itself, or that it has always existed, can be made into sentences. "The world created itself." "The world has always existed." That is easy. But to "understand" either alternative is beyond the capacity of any human mind.

If the doubters can neither answer nor understand at least one of the two questions, they have not provided a way of thinking about matter. And to really do without God or a "maker," you have to show that matter "always was," or that matter "made itself."

Then, to really <u>understand </u>the "material world," you have got to know what matter is.

No atheist or agnostic claims to know what matter is. Not even any scientist claims to know what matter is.

To truly understand what matter is, you have to know <u>how</u> and <u>why</u> it exists. No atheist, agnostic, or scientist claims to know those things. They are, and all will admit that they are, in ignorance of that "how" and "why."

So, any system of thinking that such people attempt to build must rest in, on, or over, that ignorance. And there is no rational way that ignorance can serve as, or be called a foundation for, truth. There is simply no basis for the materialistic view, or for the "scientific" definitions formed out of it.

Science, then, is a building that has no foundation.

To say that you have a "science," is to say you "know." That is what the word, science, means. But scientists <u>do not</u> "know."

And scientists are, basically, matter-men. To repeat the problem of matter-men: materialists: Either matter made itself, or it has existed forever. To do without God, the scientist must either show that matter "always was," or that "it made itself."

The scientist cannot demonstrate, or even understand, either of those two ideas. So he is faced with ideas which cannot be understood or proved, but which determine values, meanings and morality within his system. The scientist must admit to being either without understanding or to being in ignorance. He is probably both: Without understanding <u>and</u> in ignorance.

People who say that God does not exist, or that a conscious power does not exist, are only saying that they do not "know" of Him, or of the power. They do not ever say that they "know" or "can show" that He does not exist. They cannot. Because it is not possible to have positive evidence of a negative thing -- to have conclusive evidence that "something that is not, is not."

Trying to prove a negative assertion is a problem like this: Suppose that there are one billion crows in the world. All of the crows are black except one, which is white. Suppose you have a theory that there is no such thing as a white crow. How do you prove it?

You catch every single one of the billion crows and hope that, when you check, they are all black.

A man trying to prove that there was no such thing as a white crow could catch 999,999,999 black ones. By the rules of probability, at that point, the evidence is very good that no white crows exist. But then the white crow is caught. Of course that causes the conclusion based upon probability to mean nothing. The theory of the "negative" that no white crow exists fails with the finding of that single white crow.

Athiests and agnostics are like men who spend their lives catching black crows to prove that there are no white ones. Their labors and opinions in the situation mean nothing to the religious or mystical person -- like the apostle

Paul, Dr. Bucke or Walt Whitman, or even Dr. Alexis Carrell -- who has "caught a white crow."

The person who believes in God or in a Power makes a positive statement. The believer does not have any of the unsolvable problems that the materialist meets with in defending a negative conclusion.

The man who does not believe in God can only plead a <u>lack</u> of "God happening" in his life, or a <u>lack</u> of "knowing" about God.

He who <u>does</u> believe points to "God happening," to "<u>things</u> that happen," as <u>proving</u> that God is in his life. He says, "Something <u>is</u>." The believer asserts that he behaves in certain ways, and looks at things in certain ways, that <u>pay off</u> in happiness. He says, "The ways in which I act and look at things bring me love, peace, freedom and security. Here, there is a power -- and that power is a <u>giver</u> -- and I <u>know</u> that that power is a giver, <u>because I receive and enjoy the gifts</u>."

Back to my reader. Whatever the form of any previous statement, the final decision about what you will believe and what you will not believe will still be made by you. It is still up to you to finally decide what "the power" is. Now, you are simply trying to "see" it, or to see it by "feeling it."

Whatever the power is, which so many people have come to accept as being real, it must be able to give you -- in fact it identifies itself <u>by</u> giving you -- the great gifts of love, peace, freedom, and security. Those things "can be" in the universe. If they could not, we would not know them. And many, many people experience them.

If nothing but the "matter" of the materialist "is," does this mean that matter has love, peace, freedom and security built into it somehow? Does this mean that matter can think? We <u>do</u> have thoughts. But thoughts cannot be shown to be in <u>matter</u>.

Think a chair. That is, you "think" <u>of</u> a chair. And you "look" at a chair. The chair that you think, is a <u>real</u> "thought-chair." In spite of that, the thought-chair is not real "in matter" in any way that a scientist thinks of matter. Yet, your thought is a real thing. It is as real as -- perhaps more real than -- the chair that you "see."

But who cares which is the "more real?"

97

We want the "place" where love, peace, freedom and security are. Nothing in life has value without the gifts. We don't have to explain what "reality" is if the particular level or plane that we can contact gives us a means to acquire the great gifts. We are simply talking about gifts which we can feel that we actually have when we are happy.

Or, more exactly, we are talking about how we feel when we have the feeling of love; of loving or of being loved; of peace or of feeling peace; of security or of feeling secure; of freedom or of feeling free. We are talking about what may be called "mere emotions," but which will add to or take away from the "feelings" that we want to get and to keep and to make grow.

When we looked at love, perhaps the "mother" of all good feelings, we said that it can be very strong. In fact love can be so strong that it remakes both the person who loves and all of that person's world.

Back to the Golden Rule.

Suppose I told you that in order to get any one of the great gifts, you have to give the very same gift. Do you see how that is true? Do you see the "golden rule" there? Do you see the "law of reaction?"

Now, you don't necessarily have to "have" a specific great gift to "give" it. You can try to give others any great gift after "seeing" it in anyone who gives it, or who tries to give it, to you. Or you may somehow "guess" what a particular gift is, and then try to give it. If you are lucky enough to truly "feel" the great gifts, you will certainly give them to others. You will not be able to keep yourself from doing it.

So you give, to get. You want love. You must give it. This may be because you "have it" to give. Or perhaps you simply "know" how people who love, "do things." If so, then you go out and, "in cold blood," do things that way yourself. That is, go through the motions of love until you "feel love." It is just as you would repeat the moves of swimming, or of any other action you wish to learn, until you are proficient in that action.

And so, again, if you want love, you must give it. If you want peace, you must grant it. If you want freedom, you must give that. If you want security, you must give it whenever and wherever you can. And you must never disturb any such things where they already are.

You can "test" the method by giving peace, freedom and security in small ways. You will then be <u>going through</u> the best motions of <u>love</u>. For love is peaceful, freedom-giving, and secure, in itself.

Pay attention. Love has a peculiar characteristic that you should try very hard to understand. If you understand this characteristic of love, you will never feel unnecessary pain in <u>not</u> being loved.

Love has a strange way of benefiting you more whenever you have it to give than when it is given to you.

Suppose that you wanted love from a thousand people and they <u>did</u> love you. This would have its pleasant side. All of those loving people could keep you amused and more comfortable by staying around and doing things for you.

But there is no reason at all to expect that love from hundreds of people would ever make you feel what <u>they</u> feel as they love and give. You cannot have the rewards of love from <u>their</u> feeling it. You will have the rewards of love only from feeling love, yourself.

So, remember, once you have truly loved, you have been admitted into the very center of all knowledge, understandings, meanings, and values. You are then, no longer on the outside, looking in. You are on the inside, looking out. You have arrived.

And that is why I recommend "going through the motions" of giving peace, freedom and security to others as often as you can. The propagation of those gifts can also be speeded up by the reverse process of refraining from many different kinds of negative comments and actions.

Please continue to accept "for reading" that love is somehow central to the other gifts of peace, freedom, and security. Now, add the idea, also "for reading," that <u>loving behavior</u> is to be <u>imitated</u>. Add one more thing, "for reading." We <u>do not</u> have to be <u>feeling</u> love to imitate loving behavior.

Later we will look more at how giving peace, freedom and security to others meets the "rule" of love, and <u>why</u> it meets the rule. For now, let us review what peace, freedom and security may really be.

Peace will not belong to a man just because he is a millionaire, has a lot of property, and knows a lot of people. He may be able to keep thing quiet around him, and have things the way he wants them, but if his <u>mind</u> is not at peace, his <u>whole world</u> is without peace.

That a millionaire owns much property will not necessarily keep peace from him, but what he owns may make it more difficult for him to have peace. He may wish <u>too much</u> to keep everything, or may fall into self-disturbing behavior trying to get more.

However, having nothing is not a sure means to gaining peace. On the other hand, having nothing will not prevent peace from coming to you. Most of us know that having or not having peace in our lives has nothing to do with circumstances. It is easy to see that peace may be in a person's life even when the peace cannot be explained. There <u>is</u> a "peace that passeth understanding."

Here is a true story of how peace in life came to the famous Russian author, Fyodor Dostoyevsky, who wrote the novel, "Crime and Punishment."

He had been in prison for some time. He was under sentence of death. Terribly miserable and afraid, he was dreading the day that he would be executed. He was finally led out before a firing squad and blindfolded to be shot. He stood shaking, expecting at any moment to hear gunshots and to feel his body being torn by bullets.

But, then, as even real life will sometimes have it, before the order to shoot was given, the execution was halted by a last-minute note. A pardon from the Czar had been received for Dostoyevsky.

When he realized that he had been spared, so close to death, he was flooded full of great peace and relief. Then, that suddenly, he knew nothing but how wonderful if was simply to be alive. "Comfort" in life was no longer important to him. Back in his cell, he was overjoyed to find new satisfactions coming through every sense in his body. He knew joy in simply "seeing," in simply "feeling" textures, in simply "hearing" all of the common sounds and noises, in simply "smelling" the parade of odors, and in simply tasting the plainest food and drink. Bread and water became a banquet. His cold, damp, dirty straw-strewn cell seemed to him as satisfying as a room in a fancy hotel. A feeling of peace and appreciation settled on him and stayed with him all of his life. (Those feelings were probably the source of the very mystical slant that he gave to the psychology of his stories.)

I'm sure you can understand, almost feel and share, the release that Dostoyevsky had been given from many day-to-day worries. You can imagine how drastically a near-death by shooting while in prison could change the priorities of your life.

Perhaps this story shows that peace will not come to many of us unless we back off from life and take another look at it, somehow.

Probably, we need to be ready to meet the end of this life at any time; to understand that it may end at any moment. This helps us the most to measure the worth of things, and thus to know what to keep, and for how long. We should make these choices for ourselves, and sometimes for others, so that we may see clearly what one thing or aim is best. We can come to know what we want <u>most</u> in our lives -- the one and only thing which we could not (or think we could not) -- live without. When we know that, we know what to work for <u>hard</u>, and what not to work for <u>too</u> hard.

That ability to choose what is best is one meaning of Matthew, Chapter 6, verse 22, in The Bible: "The light of the body is the eye: If, therefore, thine eye be single, thy whole body shall be full of light."

You can, then, "fill your body with light" by deciding what in life is most important. Still, you realize in your heart that every physical thing will go at last upon death. You can practice the attitude of "backing off," in spirit, from everything material around you, <u>except as you use it</u>. You maintain some of the attitude about all things, all persons, that you would have if you knew that you would soon be dead. But, in the meantime, you must go on doing your "duty" to others, and enjoy as much as ever what you have to enjoy, and not be afraid to get more to enjoy. The "sorting," the "attitude," "doing your duty," and enjoying whatever you fittingly can: these are the sources of peace.

So, you decide what is of worth in life, and begin to gain inner peace. If you wish to keep that inner peace, you keep outer peace by being peaceful. If you are noisy, you will make others noisy. Whatever you do that disturbs others will come back to disturb you.

If you blame, you will be blamed. If you criticize, you will be criticized. Disrupt the schedules of others, and your schedules will be disrupted.

The tongue causes the most trouble. The tongue has incredible powers to promote good or evil. Wonderful verses of truth and warning about that are found in The Bible, James, Chapter 3:

"My brethren, be not many masters, knowing that we shall receive the greater condemnation.

2 For in many things we offend all. If any man offend not in word, the same is a perfect man, and able to bridle the whole body.

3 Behold, we put bits in the horses' mouths, that they may obey us; and we turn about their whole body.

4 Behold also the ships, which, though they be so great, and are driven by fierce winds, yet they are turned about with a very small helm, whithersoever the governor listeth.

5 Even so the tongue is a little member, and boasteth great things. Behold, how great a matter a little fire kindleth.

6 And the tongue is a fire, a world of iniquity; so is the tongue among our members, that it defileth the whole body, and setteth on fire the course of nature; and it is set on fire of hell.

7 For every kind of beasts, and of birds, and of serpents, and of things in the sea, is tamed and hath been tamed of mankind:

8 But the tongue can no man tame; it is an unruly evil, full of deadly poison.

9 With it bless we God, even the Father; and with it curse we men, made after the similitude of God.

10 Out of the same mouth cometh blessing and cursing. My brethren, these things ought not to be.

11 Doth a fountain send out at the same place sweet water and bitter?

12 Can a fig tree, my brethren, bear olive berries? either a vine, figs? so can no fountain both yield salt water and fresh.

13 Who is a wise man and endued with much knowledge among you? let him show out of good conversation his works with meekness of wisdom.

14 But if ye have bitter envying and strife in your hearts, glory not, and lie not against the truth.

15 This wisdom descends not from above, but it is earthly, sensual, devilish.

16 For where envying and strife is, there is confusion and every evil work.

17 But the wisdom that is from above is first pure, then peaceable, gentle, easy to be intreated, full of mercy and good fruits, without partiality, and without hypocrisy.

18 And the fruit of righteousness is sown in peace of them that make peace." (End quote.)

Look at security, now. Security begins to some extent when you make a habit of <u>practicing</u> peace. But security is difficult to understand. Because, in the world as it is, there is no promise that any one of us will find security as people usually think of security.

That is, most people don't want to die sooner than they think they should. They want to keep property and other "things." They would like always to have friends, skills, and to be healthy. None of these things is guaranteed.

Feeling secure involves paradox. Feeling secure is actually a state of living comfortably with insecurity. For insecurity is an "always thing," a constant, in life. You must learn to be ready for <u>any kind</u> of change in <u>anything</u> in your life. You do not have to be able <u>to predict</u> any changes. You just have to be ready to <u>put up with</u>, and deal with, change.

There is more that is hard to understand about security. And that "more" takes <u>thinking backward</u>.

We have seen that human plans and work will not give you complete security, as security is commonly wished for. But once you know that, you will see more and more what a great amount of security is "built into" the world, and identify that security by the ways that it works "in spite of" men. And then you can take comfort in it. Because you can see how that "built-in security" guards you and supports you without your having to think about it. You see the whole cycle of wind and rain and seasons and growth, their sustaining regularity. And there is all of the maintaining physiology of your body: how it uses food, acts in dangers, all of its self-protection and self-repair.

Also, there is much that we do in life that does not need all of the work and strain we put into it.

It makes no sense, when we drive a car, to tense all of our muscles and push and grunt with every turn of the wheels. That is acting as if our strength and will and directed efforts were needed to burn the gasoline and convert the pressures in the engine into the energy and mechanical motions that move the car. But if we relax and still stay alert, we get where we want to go, without strain. We are even able to watch other cars, people and external objects more effectively, to keep safe.

In the same way, it makes no sense to sweat and strain in "driving" the body, this "car of life." Keep the body in food and water, give it enough rest and mechanical care, and it does well. Pay attention, moving along the highway of "what happens." Do whatever you can "as you are," each day.

Again, to feel secure, is largely to be prepared for <u>anything</u> to happen. If you expect to unfailingly predict what will happen, you expect too much.

But security will not come to you fully until you see what <u>freedom</u> is. If you are not free, you cannot be secure.

As noted earlier, you get freedom by giving it. And, while it is easy to see how we "ought" to give it, it is very hard to give it <u>as we should</u>.

It is hardest to give freedom properly to the people whom we say we love the most. This should be the easiest, if we love truly, because true love is a freeing thing. Love should free us from others, and love should free others from us.

The freedom that we give others must be "complete," or we will not have freedom ourselves. You have your "duties," but those duties do not include thinking for anyone else, telling a person how to live, or trying to control a person. Unless that person asks for your help, or is a child, or is not competent. Even then, you must be very careful.

It is easy for you not to worry about people you do not care for. They are clearly free to be away from you. They do whatever they wish, without your advice. They live their own lives and you don't "get in their way." You behave so with them, because you really don't care what they do, say or think, as long as you are not disturbed, injured, or put to expense. You do not mind having the attitude that "it's none of my business," <u>because</u> you don't care.

With friends, with those close to you, especially with those whom you truly love, it is more difficult to feel that what they do is "none of my business." Even when they are out of sight.

But do you have the right to push into the affairs of even the person closest to you? Even by questioning, let alone by trying to control? Should not the one you love have <u>at least</u> the freedom you give to people you do not care for?

You give this freedom to one whom you love, out of trust. It should be greater than the "space" you give to people who do not interest you. You can't be free and worry about what anyone else in the world might do, say or think, out of your sight. You cannot expect to lean on somebody to "keep you steady" and "happy," and be secure.

Do you see how freedom given or denied in the personal life makes or breaks your security? Do you see that you must leave "hands off" with those you love, just as with those you do not care for?

With those whom you love, you are, naturally, not nearly as "uninterested" as you are with those for whom you do not care. With outsiders, you can have an "uncaring" disinterest. With those you love or care about, you try to maintain a more "detached" interest.

How, then, should "you" <u>act</u>? Recall all of the small ways by which others push into your affairs where they have no right to. Do they not make many unnecessary, irritating remarks? How many times do you get advice that you don't want, or get help from people which says, "You aren't doing that right," even when you are? How many times have you been laughed at, or mocked, because of what you like and don't like? And how often have you strongly felt that it was not necessary for you to explain your likes and dislikes to others?

Can you say you are good at <u>not</u> acting that way to everybody else?

If you <u>can</u> say that, you will be able to free yourself from all of the negative acts that are aimed at you. Any negatives that do happen to you simply will not have the power "to get your goat." There, is freedom.

I am trying to build a kind of flight of "golden stairs" upward using the four great gifts.

First there is the central power or effect which is <u>love</u>.

Then there is a sort of logical progression from love, to <u>peace</u>, from peace to <u>freedom</u>, and from freedom to <u>security</u>.

You might, as I said, <u>seem</u> to start with any one of the gifts. You may have love for a time without feeling peace, freedom, or security. But if you let the <u>rules</u> of love control your life, you will come into the other three great gifts so far named, plus, potentially, many more.

You must uncover love by finding out what the rules of love, or the power, are. You must <u>apply</u> those rules <u>by</u> giving peace, freedom and security to others. Then you will see how those things return to you.

Seeing the rules <u>work</u>, you will gain more insight into the things of love, or of the power. And love finally will complete this all.

Let us examine how truth is related to power. Truth is the most important element in power. So, if you wish to be in control of affairs as much as possible, you should be trying to decide <u>what</u> the <u>truth</u> is <u>to you</u>. <u>Not</u>, just now, what the truth <u>is</u>, and what you know about it. But, simply, what do <u>you believe</u> is true?

What you call <u>truth</u>, though, will have to make sense whenever you put it beside the name that you gave to <u>the power</u>. <u>Your</u> truth will be the heart of <u>your own</u> system for <u>using the rules</u> that seem to bring the four great gifts. So, what is the truth, as you define the truth, yourself, and what is the power, as you define the power, yourself?

Here is where you must be wise. And, to be wise, it may help us to know what wisdom is.

Wisdom is making everything you do "line up" with truth and love. To know the truth, is to have "facts" at hand. To love is to have "an understanding heart." To be wise, then, is to speak and act out of those facts of truth "in love."

We earlier mentioned the concept of an "inner man." What follows is intended to help us direct our thoughts in such a way as to "influence," or communicate with, that, at least theoretical, entity.

Again, do <u>not</u> make a <u>person</u> or <u>an intelligence</u> out of your "power name" unless you want to, or have come to believe that you must do so. I <u>do</u> want you to consider that some inside part of yourself may be able to help make certain changes to bring you a happier life.

Psychologists see this. They tell us to "tell ourselves," often, about the things we want to do. <u>Maxims</u> or <u>sayings</u> repeated over and over "outside" go into the "inside" thinking-life. The maxims may work there, even if we don't know they are working. This is only to say that you have <u>thought</u> and <u>life in you</u>. That is all of a "reason why" you need, in order to believe and act as though some part of the world-- the inner world -- tries to carry out the <u>rules</u> we feed into it.

Those rules go into a kind of "subjective mind," and that mind processes them into our lives. This is only common psychology. But it gives us a chance to push some of our own ideas into that deeper mind, and not let only the often stubborn and ignorant people around us push their ideas into it.

Out of what follows, please choose anything that seems like it might be a good "working rule," and put it into your own words. Don't worry if the rule comes out of The Bible, Christ, God, or some mystic. You do not have to accept The Bible, Christ, God, or mystics to make a rule work. State the rule you choose, in words of your own. But what you say must "mix well" with the "power" that you named for yourself.

Now you are near to working the rules. Because <u>knowing the rules</u> is enough to be able to make them work for you. You do not have to understand why they work. Take the rule that you make, and <u>use</u> it. Don't worry about who said it or where it came from. <u>Use it</u> and you will get the desired results.

Consider this phrase: "God is love." It is from The Bible, First John, Chapter 4, verses 8 and 16.

You may not believe that there is a God. You might not want to "fool with" the Bible. But you can, out of self-interest, take time to look at the quote.

An atheist might tend to be blinded to the phrase, "God is love," by his disbelief in God. That is, the atheist may not want to consider the idea, <u>because</u> it <u>is</u> about God.

But even an atheist should be able to see that the quotation might be an important statement <u>about love</u>, Even <u>atheists</u> know about love.

Look at the phrase, "God is love," backward.

It says that love is, somehow, the most important of all things. However, reversing the quote does not mean that "Love is God." But it could still mean that love is <u>something</u>.

And it could be important to decide what that something is for you.

Look at the phrase, "God is truth," in the same way. Reverse it to, "Truth is God." As before, we will not argue over how the phrases are different. But, either way, truth is presented as a very important idea.

Desiring truth, how, then, would <u>you</u> decide what is true in your life? What is truth? Where is truth? How is truth to be used?

Suppose that, <u>truth in you</u> gives off some <u>clue</u> or light, as a lightbulb gives off light and heat whenever electricity passes through it. Even if you don't believe in God, you must have some idea of what you believe to be true. Perhaps, if truth is in you, you should "feel" a certain way.

Consider fear and love. Love affects fear. The Bible says, "There is no fear in love; but perfect love casteth out fear." (First John; 4:18.)

As before, forget the question of God.

But, what do you know of <u>love</u>? If love were in you, how should you feel? Obviously, if "love casts out fear," if you love you should not know fear. You should not be afraid.

Love is perfect to whatever level you have it. You are free from fear to the same level that you love. God does not need to be directly in the picture when you, yourself, make judgments about the nature of love.

You probably have seen that love, even as most people inadequately experience it, "makes" many kinds of courage. You do not have to be religious to see how fear can shrink as love grows.

<u>What</u> do <u>you</u> love? Whatever you love, look into it for "the power" that you have named.

Now examine how truth and freedom interact. It is, in detecting truth, the same as it was with the last two phrases: The Bible says, "You shall know the truth, and the truth shall make you free." (St. John;8:32.)

What, then, is the sign that you have truth?

That you are free. That you "feel" free, and "know" which paths to follow to be most free.

If you do not feel free, you do not know truth.

But, for now, decide only what you believe is in you that is true.

Please allow me to remind you of what I urged you to do, or asked you to remember, while you were reading.

1. Name "the power," yourself.

2. Decide what it is that you love the most, to begin to be rid of fear.

3. Define truth, in yourself, to be free.

4. You are <u>not</u> trying to become a Christian, a Muslim, a Hindu, a Buddhist, or a mystic.

5. You <u>are</u> simply trying to borrow anything that you can from <u>any</u> of the designated systems of thought, in order to begin to use the power that you have named, or have borrowed a name for.

Section Eleven
Wisdom

What is wisdom?

We earlier defined wisdom as speaking and acting lovingly on the basis of truth. Wise judgments are made by using facts as love requires us to do.

No one who does harm is wise. No one who destroys is wise. No one who is unkind is wise. No one who says that the letter of the law is always justice is wise. (Consider, "The letter of the law killeth, but the spirit of the law giveth life." Also, "Love covereth the multitude of sins.")

Again, do not reject or be distracted by any words or quotations simply because you don't like their source or doubt their truth.

And don't just look under the words for what the person who said them believed. Look under the words of the rules to see if you can tell how a person would act who <u>did</u> believe them. That has nothing to do with religion. It only has to do with how you should behave to be happy.

Believing rightly, in love, then, is wisdom. And most people are not aware of the infinite rewards that are in wisdom. But infinite rewards, there are.

Decide whether or not you would like to be wise; whether or not you would like to be able to dip into the great treasures of wisdom. See the following:

From Proverbs; 4:5-9.

5 Get wisdom, get understanding: forget it not: neither decline the words of my mouth.

6 Forsake her not, she shall preserve thee; love her and she shall keep thee.

7 Wisdom is the principal thing -- therefore get wisdom, and with all thy getting, get understanding.

8 Exalt her, and she shall promote thee: she shall bring thee to honor, when thou dost embrace her.

9 She shall give to thine head an ornament of grace: a crown of glory shall she deliver to thee.

Proverbs; 3:13-18.

13 Happy is the man that findeth wisdom, and the man that getteth understanding.

14 For the merchandise of it is better than the merchandise of silver and the gain thereof than fine gold.

Peace, happiness and long life, then, are <u>with</u> wisdom; the ways of wisdom <u>are</u> ways of happiness.

And wisdom is in all of the open secrets.

Following, we will review three important issues.

1. Why many people believe that they cannot use the power in open secrets.

2. Why they are wrong to think that.

3. And how they <u>can</u> use that power by applying <u>proper thought and attention</u>.

We have proposed that "the power" is the source of love and truth. From love, on one side, peace and security come. And peace and security contribute to health. From truth, on the other side, freedom and authority come. And freedom and authority can be helps in gaining wealth. The line from love and the line from truth join together to produce happiness. This jointure of love and truth in a person will give him some spiritual powers. The jointure may even make him eligible to be given worldly power, as well.

Love and truth are two ways in which the power may show itself to us. (In some contexts, by the way, love is thought of as "heat," and truth is thought of as "light.")

A person who knows truth in the material world has built a kind of intellectual love in his mind. But his mental house of truth will not be a genuinely wise truth until that truth is conjoined with love in his life.

Peace and security grow out of love, because love casts out fear, and lack of fear equals security, and also peace.

Freedom and authority come from truth, since truth is freeing, and truth is the only base for authority that will work and stand "looking into."

Health is out of peace and security, from love. This is demonstrated in medicine and psychology, which show that "good emotions" promote good health. And love is the best generator of good emotions.

Wealth tends to grow out of freedom and authority from truth, because gaining wealth results from knowing "how to work" the real world and many things in it to get money and property. You cannot "know," really, without truth. But wealth can sometimes "come looking for you," simply because you think rightly.

Health and wealth are peculiar in that, while both are very desirable in themselves, neither one is necessary to happiness. And happiness is our main goal.

Happiness, then, comes out of the four great gifts, love, peace, freedom, and security. Most of us would feel complete upon finding all of these.

Power is given last place as a desirable good. It is certainly not necessary to happiness. But since it shows itself in many ways in the world, it is worth examining, at least enough to be slightly understood.

There is power, as it is used by good men. And there is power, as it is used by bad men. So, broadly, power is of two kinds.

These two kinds of power come out of opposed kinds of "authority." As we noted, the best kind of authority, the only "real" authority, comes out of truth. The baser, rather false kind of authority, comes out of the muzzle of a gun, or sheer brute force. We very often see that "brute force" at work around us. Fortunately, and more commonly than we may realize, the power of truth, the "real" power, works around us, too.

These opposed kinds of power are of two "ethical" kinds.

There is the power that builds.

And there is the power that destroys.

Broadly, again, men who build are good, and men who destroy are bad.

It is difficult even for the "good" man to be "good enough" to be safely trusted with power over others. But power will always be given to the "good" man when he becomes good enough.

The evil man will take power by force. He usually begins the process by exercising cunning. So he will use people any time he sees a chance. And he will <u>destroy</u> to get and to keep power.

Power, then, completes a step that may open itself naturally to a good man, but which can be taken by force by a bad man.

And in everyday life, power, in its types, and in the way it operates around us, affects the "general" happiness; the happiness of groups and populations.

It is all right to search until you find happiness. Everyone has a <u>right</u> to get happiness. (Our Bill of Rights is often misremembered as saying that our government is expected to <u>give</u> us happiness. In fact, the document only says that we have a <u>right</u> to <u>pursue</u> happiness.)

We do not need to go any further into studying about power and the means of acquiring it, although the person who fully understands love and truth may have all power, simply through that understanding.

Look, then, for worthy ways to chase, or pursue, happiness, and it will more surely be caught.

But let us return to the three "issues for review" that were listed just before this discussion of concepts which are related to love and truth.

1. Why many people believe that they cannot
use the power in open secrets.

2. Why they are wrong to think that.

3. And how they <u>can</u> use that power by
applying <u>proper thought and attention</u>.

You have already seen something of how to use the open secrets. Most importantly, remember that we said that <u>understanding</u> open secrets is <u>not</u> necessary to making them work. They "work" whether or not you understand them.

Please do not let any wish to "understand" keep you from trying to use the rules. Such a wish to understand is exactly what prevents a person's progress in the subjective world with which we are dealing. It is not <u>bad</u> to wish to understand. It's only bad if you give up "testing" the rules because you want to understand them first.

Besides, although the rules <u>are</u> "easy to learn," they are <u>not</u> easy "to understand."

Also, many "systems" give the rules in different words. Religion, philosophy, mysticism, and materialism, with their varying "jargons" make too many words. And, if religion, or philosophy, or mysticism, "turns you off," or you cannot accept some advice from a "worthy" materialist, this may keep you from ever knowing the rules at all. Then, too, if you insist that some specific religion is "right," you may overlook good advice from all of the other systems.

And all members of those systems see the same power that you do every day, and they all want to use it.

Do they learn how?

Most of them do, to a greater or lesser extent.

And we, you and I, want to know <u>what</u> they do to use the power.

In other words, we want <u>results</u>, not <u>reasons</u>. That is, if we can get the desired gifts by practicing certain ways of using the power, we do not need to know why the practicing works.

The wish to "understand" arises because we think we need to be able to "believe" in what we choose to do. This is like insisting that for something to work, (such as the automobile that you simply start and drive,) you must understand it, and we have seen that that is not true. So, to believe a thing, many people feel that they need to understand it. Since, wherever they don't understand, they tend not to believe, they may conclude that they do not have <u>faith</u>. They may also conclude that if they do not have faith, the rules that we are reviewing won't work for them. They feel as if faith is a sort of gasoline without which the rules cannot be run.

But that is not true. You do not need to "believe" out of understanding. You do not need that kind of faith. You do not have to be able to say, "I understand, thus I believe, and thus I have faith." This search for faith only stands in the way of a try or trial of the rules.

What about faith? There are a number of kinds. Let's talk about two.

First is the faith that most of us think of as "religious faith." It is a faith that can "believe" <u>without</u> knowing or being taught anything. Such faith may come to a person from what he thinks was a touch of God in his life. Such faith may begin with a "mystical change," like that of Doctor Bucke, Walt Whitman, or the apostle Paul. This mystical change is, of course, not common.

The other kind of faith is the kind that we want.

This is the kind of faith that a man "builds" for himself. And he builds it because he has decided that it will promote his happiness to do so.

And then, as a means of becoming happy, he will further decide to hold on to this constructed faith with both hands and apply it to his own thoughts and actions.

We need to "make" a "faith" <u>with our minds</u> -- and then we must <u>bring in our will-power</u> to use that faith.

We must think like this:

"I see that there are many true things that I do not understand. This does not keep me from believing them, because they are in my experience. I know them, and I know their processes and I accept their uses, but I still do not understand them.

"Suppose I can't believe a thing because I do not understand it. My not believing it does not <u>make</u> it false. I have believed some things to be false that I found out were true, so believing is not the test.

"I want a happy life; love, peace, freedom and security, the great gifts. I see that I cannot buy, trap or steal them. No one can <u>give</u> them to me. No one sells them. No businessman stocks them. Yet, everyone wants the great gifts. But no one can guarantee a way to get them. Everyone tries to explain, but everyone seems to have a 'different story.' This may mean that no one has it 'quite right.' Worse, <u>all</u> may be wrong.

"But, wait.

"All of the explainers <u>agree</u> on the <u>rules</u>.

"Well then, if the rules are so special, I'll look at them myself. I'll forget about 'explanations.' Then I can put the rules to work in my own way."

Still talking to yourself, you say, "I need a 'specialist.' If I want to know about the law, I go to a lawyer, a specialist in law. For medical advice, I go to a doctor, a specialist in medicine. I willingly pay for specialists' services because I expect that they will know what to do in their specialties. They have training and experience that I do not.

"I do not argue with them about <u>what</u> they do or <u>why</u> they do it. I have my own skills -- my "own store to keep." I can't do their jobs too.

"If I sell my own skills, and I do my own jobs well, I will be trusted. I don't have to explain to my customers how much I know, or always give each of them reasons for what I do. If I can't have their trust, I don't want their business.

"Well, I want happiness. Then I want a 'specialist in happiness:' in love, peace, freedom and security.

"Such specialists have varied titles. Some are called philosophers. Some, preachers. Some are monks, mystics, Zen Buddhists, missionaries. Some are positive thinkers, psychologists, or psychotherapists.

"But each of these specialists in happiness brings with him a whole forest of words.

"Now, I want to see what they are all talking about without getting mixed up in their arguments. I want to save years of time.

"How?

"I'll hear them all. Then I'll pick out what they all say it is important to do.

"And I will not pick out only what I can believe. But what ALL of the specialists agree upon, I will treat as important. That way, I won't get bogged down in all of the different reasons they have for using the words that they use." (Here, you stop talking.)

Now you just need to decide to follow the rules.

It will be easy, since you will write them all down.

Then you say, "I see what the rules tell me to do. I can 'make up my mind' to give them a try."

Section Twelve
Why Try The Rules?

Because you want love, peace, freedom and security. You want to be happy.

But you will not get the great gifts without trading for them.

And the one and only thing you can trade, is an <u>effective attitude</u>. Which is, a "way of looking at things" <u>that works</u>.

Also, if you want to use the rules, be sure that you know <u>why</u> you want to use them. And those various motivations will not be the usual "highly moral" ones, but will include the more negative motivations which we will go over again, right now.

Your "why" for trying the rules will <u>not</u> be because you want to "make this a better world." It will <u>not</u> be because you feel that you must help your fellow man. It will <u>not</u> be because you want to save your soul from hell. And it will <u>not</u> be because you want to be <u>good</u>.

Perhaps you will wish all of those things someday, maybe even now, incidentally. But many of us are not far enough along on this path of improvement to follow the rules for those reasons.

Of course, you will need to follow rules which tell us to help others.

Only, <u>you</u> will follow the rules because it helps <u>you</u>.

But you will need to overcome the usual resistance that people have to taking advice. You could make a list of areas of concern in which most of us will not, or can not, put good advice into practice. The first area is probably the most familiar, and it has to do with controlling one's weight. Other areas involve the use of alcohol and cigarettes and illicit drugs, which are all harmful. But few of the people injured by those things are much affected by any counsel about them, and will not take action until it becomes clear that if they do not, they will soon be dead.

You probably know that to overcome personal problems, you must really <u>want to do it</u>. Some of the barriers to gaining the great gifts are like those against ending bad habits affecting your health.

If you want to be happy, you must make up your mind to do what is needed to be happy.

Let us assume that you have made up your mind. Then understand this: You cannot get to happiness by a direct road. You have to make subtle mental adjustments to use a few short detours as you travel. You need to recognize another condition that must be met to reach happiness.

Change yourself, and happiness comes <u>to</u> you.

You have seen that happiness keeps company with certain "great gifts." We have named four of those gifts, love, peace, freedom, and security. And now you want to get them in order to be happy.

You decide that you can get the great gifts by giving them. Then you try to give them.

You might only be able to do a little giving each day. But what you do give, you will see a reward for. And when you see the reward for giving the gifts, you will be able to give them more easily. Further, when the rewards grow plain, you will begin to have a "faith" that can only come from the "trying to give."

But you must try long enough. You are not likely to find the "quick" Aladdin's Lamp, though you might. Usually, you will need to work with the "slower" Aladdin's Lamp.

Besides, you must learn how to "rub" the lamp.

The rule, the "how to rub," is: What you give will return to you. If harmony, security, peace and freedom are not in your life, you need to check and see what you are giving out every day. The law cannot fail. You get back your own kind of coin. And this does not apply only to good deeds. It applies to every harmful, or merely thoughtless action of negative impact, as well.

Compare the process of reward from giving the great gifts to putting money in a bank. When you have deposited a thousand dollars to savings, you expect to receive interest in return. Before that, as with behaving rightly in order to be happy, you decided to deposit the money, and you deposited it.

But do you come back in twenty-four hours and demand your five- or six-percent interest?

No.

You did make the deposit. But you know that some period of time set by law will have to pass before you can get your interest.

So, what happens if you grow angry because you are not paid off <u>right now</u>, and you take your money out? You would lose the sure return that time and patience would bring.

It is much the same with love, peace, freedom and security. You must make deposits. You must expect time to pass for interest to build up. Thankfully, the more you invest, the more you get back.

The return, here, is more certain than a return of gold. The return is even better than gold. And there is no limit to the interest you can get. In fact, whatever you give, the return will even be multiplied.

And when love, peace, freedom and security are properly laid claim to, they will never leave you, in spite of anything that can happen to you. ANYTHING.

But a FAKE faith may be needed for some people. We spoke before about constructing a kind of "intellectual faith" with regard to abstract matters by deliberately dismissing a need "to understand" a concept in order to believe it. That construction was done so that we might examine certain concepts directly and without distractions. We temporarily grant that an apparently untrue concept may actually be true, in order to avoid having our perceptions clouded by prejudgments.

In the same way, here, we regard the rules having to do with the great gifts as being true, beforehand. Having accepted them as true, as part of testing them, you then use them long enough to decide, from their rewards, whether or not they prove themselves, whether or not they work.

You do this by making up your mind to act upon a "made-up" faith. Again, if you please, a fake faith. Then you act upon a "faith" that was built by your mind. Because you want to be happy, in love, peace, freedom, and security.

And you do it for your own good -- not because you want to save the world.

You must, for a time, be a hypocrite. You will be a "conscious hypocrite." You will have made up your mind to act as if something is true whether or not you can believe it. You are looking for rewards. You are not trying to become a speech-maker about why you do what you do.

The usual sort of hypocrite pretends to have "goodness" or other qualities he does not have, so that he may appear to be whatever he wishes. He does not believe in whatever he pretends to think or act from. He may not even think that it is possible to believe in such bases of action and thought. He has no desire to believe it. He maintains a false front. This kind of hypocrite is one who looks as if he is good when, really, he thinks and does evil.

You should be another kind of hypocrite.

For your own happiness, be the kind of hypocrite who has decided to test that being good and doing good will get you rewards just as surely as money in savings in the bank will get you interest. More surely. And those rewards will be better than money will ever be.

You will not be evil inside, as the real hypocrite is. You may not do good in the way that the open secrets say you should do. You may think, wrongly, that you must be a "do-gooder" and "enjoy" it.

That is not true. You do not have to do good "from the heart" to get the return, any more than you have to be a do-gooder or to have true faith.

Here is a little story which shows how to be the kind of hypocrite last described.

"The Story of the Mask.

"Once upon a time, there was a very evil and very ugly man who bought a beautiful mask to wear in order to fool people so that they would love and trust him.

"The mask was so beautiful, people did love him. So much so, that, little by little, he, too, learned to love and trust people.

"Gradually, he became less and less evil, until he was a very saintly man.

"When he died, his friends discovered that he had on a mask.

"They took it off, and, lo and behold, his face had become even more beautiful than the mask!"

Think how much that man must have been changed for the better, by hypocrisy. Imagine how the good kind of hypocrisy could change your life and make it happy. You use the "fake faith" to be a "fake hyprocrite," and look for love, peace, freedom, and security, even though you may have had no experience of them, and which you may even think are not real.

Now, please allow me to recommend a way for you to maintain confidence that love, peace, freedom and security are attainable to you.

It is by reading. But reading a certain type of literature. Such reading could be thought of as "reading for fuel." The "fuel" is of an abstract kind that can be burned to power an engine of hopefulness within you.

In that burning, your mind is used. And your will-power.You could go looking in places where you have never looked, and read where you have never read.

The suggested readings will be varied. Some are the reports of people who foresaw the future. Others tell of communications with the seemingly surviving spirits of dead persons. Still others detail the work of psychics, or give the findings of some psychological researchers. Some tell of persons who apparently have a gift for "reading" all sorts of people and events.

The people referred to are not without recognition. They are not insane. They are not fakes or charlatans or liars. They report unusual happenings as plainly as they can, and they deserve a reading.

At the very end of this paper, I have placed a list of books containing such unusual material. I am suggesting that you read some of those books. I will tell you why.

Daily, you get bad news, pain and discouragement out of the material world and the "matter-minded" people around you. There is more than enough negative information and example to destroy happiness many times over. And you get it ninety-nine percent of the time.

Use a small part of that little one-percent of time left over to cancel out the poison of the ninety-nine percent. Do that by reading reports of what happens (apparently) on other levels of experience. Especially because those levels may be where the four great gifts come from. See if you do not enjoy exploring in areas where you might not have looked.

It may possibly help you to start that "look around" if you realize, as before stated, that anyone who cannot believe that the universe "was made" has to claim either that it made itself or that it has always been. That the universe made itself or always was are both ideas not understandable. Because both seem to be impossible.

That the universe has a creator may not be understandable and seem to be impossible, too. All you can say is that NO ONE OF THE THREE IDEAS MAKES ANY MORE SENSE THAN THE OTHERS.

But, for your testing of ways to behave to get the great gifts, you do not need to know which of those three inunderstandable ideas is correct. You don't even have to choose one.

Even if Jesus or the great moral teachers had never lived, life would soon show us that we get back whatever we give. The third law of motion, that for every action there is an equal and opposite reaction, would still be true.

Let me also repeat that there is no reason to regard a concept as being false simply because we do not understand it. Again, there are many ideas we know are true that we do not understand. The world is <u>here</u>, for one thing. It exists. We cannot say how it exists. We do not really understand its nature. But we do "know" it is there. We do not say, "I don't understand the world, so it isn't there."

The idea was also advanced earlier that science has within its doctrines and theories contradictions that do not appear to bother scientists very much.

But human beings are not intelligent enough in some areas of thought to know when we are dealing with real contradiction and when we are not: to know if two ideas will "mix" or not.

Suppose we are dealing with two ideas that we want to say are each true. Our minds, however, cannot see how both could be true. We are dealing with what looks like a contradiction.

For example, we say on one hand that the world is all "matter" and everything in it must have a "matter" cause. But on the other hand we wish to believe that we have "free will;" that our will is not bound by material causal law. We cannot see how both things can be true.

Yet scientists base science upon, and operate upon, the assumption that "everything" is matter "in some way," and that everything that happens has a material cause.

Scientists, however, see nothing wrong with also assuming, in spite of the "laws" of science, that their thinking is not causally bound. They believe that they <u>think</u> "free." But how can logic free the conclusions of scientists from the very laws of material causality that are the basis of science?

And here is a possible solution to the dilemma. We might not, as human beings, have any way of knowing that there really is contradiction between two ideas, or sets of ideas, where we think we see contradiction. What we "see" as contradiction may only mark the limits of our ability to think or know. Contradiction may merely be a sort of illusion in the mind.

So keep testing. All of the immediately-preceding speculation is to justify asking you to never stop testing the open secrets, or the rules, simply because you come upon ideas that you think cannot go together. Do not stop testing because you believe you see a contradiction, and then think you must resolve that contradiction. If you do stop, you will have missed the point of the testing.

And what is the point of the testing? There are <u>points</u>, and they are numerous. Some, follow:

You want happiness, and you want it whether or not you can understand it. What would you care about explaining your happiness if you were happy?

I would not refuse to go into heaven simply because I had never believed it existed. I would jump through the door. I doubt that any atheist would refuse to go into heaven merely because he was angry to find out that there was one. I think that he would run right in.

It would be interesting, though, would it not, to watch the atheist furiously readjusting his ideas. He would certainly have a lot of mental reorganizing to do.

But we need not waste time arguing. You simply look for, and try to "feel," the "real" in statements like this: ... "The peace of God, which passeth understanding, shall keep your hearts and minds ... "

Forget, for a time, if it is so, that you do not believe in God. It is more important to recognize that there <u>is</u>, in this world, such peace with some people. Those who have it show it, and swear on it that they do have it. There truly is, a peace that passeth understanding. What do you care about where such peace comes from, if you have it? Look at the <u>doughnut</u> of peace that there is. Don't argue about the <u>hole</u> of explanation.

In the same way, no matter what you think of Jesus, what did he mean, or what might he have meant, when he said, "Peace I leave with you, my peace I give unto you." Jesus added, of his giving peace, " ... Not as men give do I give unto you, but as my Father in heaven giveth."

How does the world, or how do men, give or not give peace?

If you need the world to be at peace to have peace, will you ever have peace?

No.

So, if you wish to be at peace, it will have to be <u>in spite of the world</u>. Many people do, too, have peace in spite of the noise and the madness of the world.

Your best hope, then, is not to argue for or against Christ, or for or against God. Your best hope is to keep your mind on the "peace test:" to find and test the rules of peace.

You allow the rules to "soak" into your life. Simply enjoy the good of them. Then, though you may not understand the rules of peace, you can still <u>give</u> peace, and any other great gift in the same way.

Use will-power. Your test must be a "mind-aim" backed up by your "will-power." You imitate loving behavior as you "see" it in the rules. You do good, as the rules say, any time you can. You follow any rule "on purpose." With effort. Even if you are a cynic.

You "put on the beautiful mask," as in the story.

It is necessary to learn to control the emotions, in order to enjoy fully the gifts of love, peace, freedom, and security. A way of controlling the emotions is offered in our <u>second most important statement</u>. We will soon talk about that.

But I gave you earlier what I said was the <u>most important idea of all</u> to remember and to think about as you go along. And you were asked, would you be able, or not be able, to follow any suggestions given?

In connection with that, we talked about the "philosophers' stone," and how it could bring you all good things, and could change the bad to the good. You were asked to carry that statement with you, and try to "figure it out" in the context of your own life. The actual statement that I asked you not to forget was: THE TRUE PHILOSOPHERS' STONE IS LOVE. It is easy to remember.

I will give you a statement that is almost as important as that about the philosophers' stone. Without using this next statement, it is more difficult to make the philosophers' stone of love work. And I am going to ask you to test this new statement, also.

If you choose not to make the suggested test, do, always, remember that THE TRUE PHILOSOPHERS' STONE IS LOVE. And see, as well as you can, how life will, or will not, prove that statement true, if you stand upon it in your actions.

But the new statement, as I said, will help you to use the rules, to test them, much more easily than if you did not have it and remember it.

The new statement has to do with CONTROL. You must come to know that you can keep feelings like anger, envy, hate, or spite, out of your mind. You can begin to do this by telling yourself that you do not want them there because they do hurt you. They hurt you, as we saw in medical research, as truly as can a knife, a club, or a bullet.

There is something silly about bad emotions. They usually come from what we think "other people" think of us ... not from what we think of ourselves. But we must be sure enough "of ourselves" to "judge ourselves." We must not try to live by the judgments of others.

You can see how ridiculous would be any effort to conform our lives to what other people think of us. We cannot mold our behavior to the judgments of others when each other person can think something different about us. Especially when that "other person" is not very likely to "know" anything about us at all.

And here, we introduce the idea of a "switch" for the feelings. This idea is, that there is a switch that can be used to control "feelings." And, that you do not have to let that switch turn on.

You can plug a lamp into a timer, and the lamp will come on at any time you set. But you can keep the lamp from coming on, if you wish. You simply do not let it switch on. You cancel the setting of the timer.

Similarly, you can find and use the switch to your emotions, with a little effort. You can learn to "feel" that switch beginning to flip, and stop it right there. That way, you can stop emotions that are not good for you. You feel the switch start to snap on, and you stop it -- at once. This can really be a matter of life or death.

Would not such "switch-control" be very useful? It would keep you from "blowing your top."

Some of you might say, "Why, I thought it was necessary to our emotional health to 'let off steam,' to show others how we feel."

But see what a physician of long experience, Dr. John A. Schindler, says in his valuable book, "How To Live 365 Days A Year."

"Regarding the 'value' of 'blowing your top.' There is a school of psychiatrists who think that 'blowing one's top' is a good way to work off something bad. This is a view that is held by psychiatrists who cannot control their own tops.

"There is nothing to it. Blowing one's top serves no good purpose; one blowing more firmly sets the habit for the next blowing. .... Children blow their tops; it is a childish adult who finds it necessary to do so."

Back to you. In controlling the emotions, you use the rule to not do anything to anyone that would make you feel bad if someone did it to you. You must not do such things, whether or not other people do them to you. That is no excuse to behave the wrong way -- which is any way that you would not like to be treated.

Let's look at a statement related to the previous one about there being a "switch to any emotion."

THERE IS A LITTLE DELAY OR PAUSE
AT THE START OF ANY EMOTION
THAT CAN BE USED TO STOP THAT EMOTION

And the way to use that pause to stop any negative emotion, is this:

Look at the emotion as it shows itself small at the beginning. Look at your anger, or whatever it is. Do not be "in" it. If you look at the emotion, you can refuse to be drawn into it. And you must not enter.

Why?

Because any negative emotion is just like a rattlesnake. If you see a rattlesnake, you do not go on and pick it up simply because you might think yourself to be a coward if you did not, or because your friends or any onlookers might think you were a coward.

If you saw a real rattlesnake as close to you as you saw the rattlesnake of your anger, what would you do? Unless you had a very pressing reason to put yourself in danger, you would try to get away from the snake, or get it away from you ... possibly trap it, somehow.

You can learn to do the same with any emotion that you decide is poisonous. And any emotion that makes you irritable, unstable, ill, or unfriendly to others, is poisonous -- truly poisonous. You should recognize such emotions as the deadly snakes they are. And you back off.

Again, THERE IS A LITTLE DELAY OR PAUSE AT THE START OF ANY EMOTION THAT CAN BE USED TO STOP THAT EMOTION.

Take care of yourself. Use that pause. Even if at first you cannot easily sense it. It is the only moment you have to take a saving "step back."

Take that "back-step." Don't waste any time <u>looking</u> for the "click" or the "pause" in which you can take the step to the rear. (You <u>will</u> learn to "feel" the pause, and to then stop in it.)

Back off from those emotional rattlesnakes, then. It will get easier with practice. It will get easier, too, if you come to see clearly that many of the emotions you could "let run" really <u>are</u> like the worst poisonous snakes.

In that connection, remember Dr. Selye's study of stress. Remember how stress -- "bad" feelings or emotions -- destroys your body tissues as surely as snake poison does.

The two key statements here, to use and to watch work with each other, then, are:

THE TRUE PHILOSOPHERS' STONE IS LOVE.

THERE IS A LITTLE DELAY OR PAUSE
AT THE START OF ANY EMOTION
THAT CAN BE USED TO <u>STOP</u> THAT EMOTION.

Section Thirteen
Reminders, Methods, And Suggestions

Once more, below, are the four ideas presented early in this book, that were to be kept in mind while reading.

We will add to those four ideas the "two important" statements just made at the end of the last section.

We will repeat the notion that the various codes we looked at should be used as a kind of <u>verbal</u> "reading glasses." It is good to "wear the code-glasses" at chosen times to <u>practice</u> looking at the world in their way.

Back to the four ideas to be kept in mind while reading this book.

1. You remember that the rules work whether or not you believe or understand them in the usual ways.

2. You use a made-up, "fake" faith to follow the rules because you have determined to do so.

3. You remind yourself that we follow the rules because it is good for our bodies, for our health.

4. You accept, to test, that simply following the rules will help you to gain the four great gifts of love, peace, freedom, and security.

Soon, we will revisit the five most complete codes, agreeing that they contain all of the important open secrets, or rules to action, for good life and health.

But first let's examine the most important general approaches to the rules.

Recall Jesus being asked by a lawyer of the Pharisees to state the great commandment in the law. Jesus said, "Thou shalt love the Lord thy God with all thy heart, and with all thy soul, and with all thy mind. This is the first and great commandment. And the second is like unto it. Thou shalt love thy neighbor as thyself. On these two commandments hang all the law and the prophets."

Look at, "Thou shalt love thy neighbor as thyself." This is the part you work through. It would not be the part to work through for any person who knows God directly. But most of us know God indirectly. So we must work through the neighbor to demonstrate enlightenment. This was the, at least, implied point of the poem, "Abou Ben Adhem," by Leigh Hunt.

The poem's point about extending love to your fellowman must be emphasized. Because, for a person who does not believe in God, working through the neighbor is the <u>only</u> way he can test the open secrets and rules.

More generally, you must approach any rule in a way that looks <u>behind</u> or <u>under</u> the words, attempting to see the "way of acting" to which it gives clues. In that process, you need to work on getting rid of hate, ill will, and envy. Such feelings truly do damage you inside. You cannot have them without suffering their bad effects.

Consider the irony of this statement: You hate someone whom you wish could be hurt by your thoughts, then you learn that they carry on in prosperity and good health while you are becoming ill because of <u>your feelings</u> toward them. This <u>is</u> the way it happens.

For the same reason, you forgive yourself. You must not have any negative feelings about yourself. <u>Stop</u> and forgive <u>your self</u> for anything you hold against yourself. Say aloud, "I <u>do</u> forgive myself. Say aloud, "I <u>do</u> have a right to be here."

Further, you have a right to be, or not to be, anything you choose. But in making such choices, realize that you often are, also, automatically choosing to walk a positive or a negative path, choosing good or evil.

Also, in making such choices, you are determining your own worth. Remember, no other person gives you your worth. No other person can take it away. Then you <u>are</u> your own worth, <u>if</u> you acknowledge worth in others. So, be kind to yourself, and be kind to everyone else.

Soon we will revisit the six readings that contain open secrets, or rules to action, for a good life.

But before we return to the six readings which we use as "codes," let us review the five other ideas that have guided our reading:

1. The codes were to be used as kinds of
<u>eye-glasses through which we look at</u>
<u>the world</u>.

2. You did decide to test the codes.

3. You understood "why" you made that decision.

4. We described a sort of "invented faith" that was
built by the mind.

5. We introduced the codes, or rules, themselves,
beginning with the poem, "My Symphony" and
ending with the "Tao" of Lao Tze.

Keeping in mind those five guiding ideas, please look with me at four even earlier points, as they were given in their sections.

I. You were to delay until the end deciding whether any statement
you read is true or false.

II. You were only to consider whether or not you could follow any
suggestions as a test.

III. a. You were to choose your own name for the central "power"
which makes everything work.

b. You were to accept, as a test, that your body has an inner man or self that sees and remembers everything in your life.

c. You were to accept, for trial, that you can be made sick, even die, from keeping "bad" feelings in your mind.

d. You were to accept, that "good" emotions keep you healthy.

IV. a. You were to consider, that your "inside" self is the most real thing in the world.

b. And, that, because that inner you is the most real of all things, whatever it can "know" is the next most real of all things.

c. And if, b., last above, is true, then love, peace freedom, and security can be more real than anything in science; even more real than the <u>outside</u> "sticks and stones."

d. Because that inside, most real, world has the same laws as science, you must use the golden rule to be healthy and happy. (And that is why you decided to make this test, understanding that failure to obey the golden rule has even worse penalties inside than out.)

Here, we add the "Two most important statements" to the four main ideas just reviewed.

V. THE TRUE PHILOSOPHERS' STONE IS LOVE AND LOVE IS THE <u>SAME</u> AS THE <u>POWER</u> TO WHICH YOU GAVE A NAME.

VI. THERE IS A LITTLE PAUSE AT THE START OF ANY EMOTION THAT CAN BE USED TO STOP THAT EMOTION.

VII. The codes, "My Symphony," DESIDERATA, "The Persian Rosary," the Thirteenth Chapter of Corinthians, "The Way," or "TAO," and "Abou Ben Adhem," are to be "reading-glasses." They are put on for "use" <u>by being read</u>.

VIII. The rules, or codes, work whether or not you believe, understand, or have faith in them in the usual ways.

IX. You <u>make up</u> a "faith" with your mind. That faith is that you will follow the rules <u>because</u> you made up your mind to do so. The reason you do so, further, is that you want the four great gifts of love, peace, freedom, and security. You also follow the rules because doing so is good for your body and mind. It keeps you healthy.

If you read again, slowly and receptively, the six codes, My Symphony ... and so forth ... I trust that you will feel a beneficial symmetry in this book. I repeat the codes.

My Symphony

To live content with small means;
To seek elegance rather than luxury,
and refinement rather than fashion;
To be worthy, not respectable,
and wealthy, not rich;
To study hard, think quietly,
talk gently, act frankly;
To listen to stars and birds,
to babes and sages with open heart;
To bear all cheerfully, do all bravely,
await occasions, hurry never;
In a word, to let the spiritual,
unbidden and unconscious,
grow up through the common --
This is to be my symphony.

Desiderata

Go placidly amid the noise and haste and remember what peace there may be in silence. As far as possible without surrender be on good terms with all persons. Speak the truth quietly and clearly; and listen to others, even the dull and ignorant; they too have their story.

Avoid loud and aggressive persons, they are vexing to the spirit. If you compare yourself with others, you may become vain and bitter; for always there will be greater and lesser persons than yourself. Enjoy your achievements as well as your plans.

Keep interested in your own career, however humble; it is a real possession in the changing fortunes of time. Exercise due caution in your business affairs; for the world is full of trickery. But let this not blind you to what virtue there is; many persons strive for high ideals; and everywhere life is full of heroism.

Be yourself. Especially, do not feign affection. Neither be cynical about love, for in the face of all aridity and disenchantment it is perennial as the grass.

Take kindly the counsel of years, gracefully surrendering the things of youth. Cultivate strength of spirit to shield you in sudden misfortune. But do not distress yourself with imaginings. Many fears are born of fatigue and loneliness. Beyond a wholesome discipline be gentle to yourself.

You are a child of the universe, no less than the trees and the stars; you have a right to be here. And whether or not it is clear to you, no doubt the universe is unfolding as it should.

Therefore be at peace with God, whatever you conceive Him to be, and whatever your labors and aspirations, in the noisy confusion of life keep peace with your soul. Thus you will have peace everywhere.

Despite its sham, drudgery and broken dreams, it is still a beautiful world. Be careful. Strive to be happy.

A Persian Rosary

1. Love and serve humanity.

2. Praise every soul -- If you cannot praise him, let him pass out of your life.

3. Dare, dare, and then -- dare more.

4. Do not imitate. Be original. Be inventive. Be yourself -- know yourself. Stand your own ground.

Do not lean on the borrowed staff of others. Think
your own thoughts.

5. There is no saint without a past. There is no sinner
without a future.

6. See God and good in every face. All the perfections
of the Deity are concealed in you. Reveal them. The
Saviour also is in you. Let his grace emancipate you.

7. Be cheerful. Be courteous. Be a dynamo of
irrepressible happiness. Assist everyone. Let your
life be like unto a rose; though silent, it speaks in
the language of fragrance. You are a trine of body,
mind, and soul. The food of the soul is Divine Love.
Therefore feed your soul on Divine Love -- so that
the body and mind be invigorated.

8. Be deaf and dumb concerning the faults of others.
Do not listen to gossip. Silence the talebearer with
virtuous conversation.

9. Stop the circulation of the venomous germs of
religious fanaticism through your veins and arteries
and those of your children. Never argue with anyone
about his religious beliefs. Religious controversies
lead to hatred and separation. Religion is love and
fellowship, not theological dogmas and creeds.
When you have Love and Sympathy in your heart for
your fellowmen, you possess the highest type of
religion, no matter by what name you call yourself.
Rest assured that the emancipation of the world is
through the Nameless God of Love and in the
Nameless Religion of Love.

10. Develop the qualities of essential goodness. Every
soul is endowed with the attributes of intrinsic
beauty. Discover those attributes and hold them
before the world.

11. Religion is a personal relationship between man

and his maker. For God's sake don't interfere with
it, do not organize it, neither try to reduce it to so
many statements. Organization, in whatever form,
is the deathknell of religion. Do not preach this.
Practice and teach it. Let no one dictate to you
regarding what you should or should not do or
believe in your spiritual life. The final authority is the
Authority of the Spirit within you, and not that of any
man, dead or alive. The unerring withness is
standing in the center of your being -- all-powerful,
mighty and supreme! His is the final testimony. His
is the court of last appeal.

12. God's love is in you and for you. Share it with
others through association. Do not court separation
with creatures but unite with them in love. To know
yourself through your fellow men is to know God.

13. Have courage. Realize your divine origin. You are
the ray of the Sun of Immortal Bliss. You and the
Father are one. The undying radiant Self is in you.
Reverence your celestial station. No harm will ever
come to you. God's perfect image you are, abiding
in the fort of His protection. Association with all
people will lead to spiritual unfoldment and not to
the deterioration of the soul. Live above the world of
faith and infidelity; religion and atheism, orthodoxy
and Liberalism; truth and error, angel and devil;
and you will be living with and in God ... The God of
Absolute Good, the God of Absolute Beauty, the
God of Absolute Perfection.

14. In religion there is no compulsion. The path to inner
unfoldment is not by restrictions and constraints;
not by anathema and excommunication, but by
constant progress from world to world, from star to
star, from constellation to constellation forever and
without end.

15. The light of lights is in your heart. Uncover it and
let it beam for the illumination of mankind. Do not

expect a favor from friend or foe, and you shall
never be disappointed.

16. Overcome malice, envy, personal spite and
prejudice, and you are the master of destiny.

17. Do not condemn a single soul. In condemning him,
you are condemning yourself. Never for an instant
forget that he is also a child of God. Upon the great
sea of spirit, there is room for every sail. In the
limitless sky of truth there is room for every wing.

18. Do not murder the character of a soul under the
guise of religion, either by bitter blame or faint
praise. Spiritual murder is worse than taking a
man's life. Have a sin-covering eye. See only the
beautiful and the noble.

19. Be gentle. Be lenient. Forgiving. Be generous.
Be merciful. Be thoughtful. Positive. Soar in the
atmosphere of freedom. Walk in your chosen
path and let no criticism disturb you in the least.
This is the way to success, to happiness, to
health, to prosperity, to glory. Let me walk in it
all of my life.

Chapter 13 of First Corinthians

Though I speak with the tongues of men and of the angels and have not
love, I am become as sounding brass or a tinkling cymbal.

And though I can prophesy, and understand all mysteries, and am great in
all knowledge, and though I have the gift of faith, and can move mountains,
and have not love, I am nothing.

And though I give up all my worldly goods to feed the poor, and though
I give my body to be burned, and have not love, it profiteth me nothing.

Love suffers long, and is kind; love does not envy. Love is not boastful,
and love is not proud.

Love behaves acceptably. Love does not crave to own anything. Love is always calm, except for her own sake, then is slow to anger. Love contains no evil.

Love turns from wickedness, rejoices in the truth.

Love bears all things, believes all things, hopes all things, endures all things.

Love never fails: but prophecies shall fail; tongues shall cease; and knowledge shall vanish away.

And faith, hope, and love, these three, shall last forever.

But the greatest of these is love.

The Tao
by Lao Tze

Scholars of the highest class, when they hear
about the Tao, earnestly carry it into practice.
Scholars of the middle class, when they have
heard about it, seem to keep it now and then.
Scholars of the lowest class, when they have
heard of it, laugh greatly at it.

The sage puts his own person last, and yet it is
found in the foremost place; He treats his own
person as if it were foreign to him, and yet that
person is preserved. Is it not because he has no
private ends that therefore such ends are realized?
He is free from self-display, therefore he shines;
he is free from self-assertion, therefore
distinguished; free from self-boasting and
therefore his merit is acknowledged; free from
self-complacency, and therefore he acquires
superiority.

It is because the sage is free from striving that therefore no one in the world is able to strive with him. There is no guilt greater than to sanction ambition; no calamity greater than to be discontented with one's lot; no fault greater than the wish to be getting.

To those who are good (to me) I am good; and to those who are not good (to me) I am also good; and thus (all) get to be good. To those who are sincere (with me) I am sincere; and to those who are not sincere (with me) I am also sincere; and thus (all) get to be sincere.

He who has within himself abundantly the attributes (of the Tao) is like an infant. Poisonous insects will not sting him, fierce animals will not seize him; birds of prey will not strike him.

I have three precious things which I prize and hold fast. The first is gentleness; then, economy; the third is shrinking from taking precedence of others. Gentleness is sure to be victorious, even in battle, and firmly to keep its ground. Heaven will save its possessor, by his very gentleness protecting him.

Abou Ben Adhem

Abou Ben Adhem (may his tribe increase!)
Awoke one night from a dream of peace,
And saw, within the moonlight of his room,
Making it rich, and like a lily bloom,
An angel writing in a book of gold --
Exceeding peace had made Ben Adhem bold,
And to the presence in his room he said,
"What writest thou?" -- The vision raised its head,
And with a look made all of sweet accord
Answered, "The names of those who love the Lord."

"And is mine one?" said Abou. "Nay, not so,"
Replied the angel. Abou spoke more low,
But cheerfully still; and said, "I pray thee, then,
Write me as one who loves his fellow-men."

The angel wrote, and vanished. The next night
It came again with a great wakening light,
And showed the names whom love of God had blessed,
And, lo, Ben Adhem's led all the rest.

For readers who could use a more prayer-like affirmation,
the following may be read daily, or as you decide.

AFFIRMATION

I am a center in the Divine Mind, a point of
God-Conscious life, truth and action. My affairs are
divinely guided into right action, into correct results.
Everything I do, say or think, is stimulated by the
Truth. There is power in the word that I speak,
Because it is of the Truth, and it is the Truth. There is
perfect and continuous right action in my life and my
affairs. All belief in wrong action is dispelled and
made negative. Right action alone has power, and
right action is power, and Power is God -- the Living
Spirit Almighty. This spirit animates everything that I
do, say or think. Ideas come to me daily, and these
ideas are divine ideas. They direct me and sustain
me without effort. I am continuously directed. I am
compelled to do the right thing at the right time, to
say the right word at the right time, to follow the right
course at all times.

All suggestions of age, poverty, limitation or
unhappiness are uprooted from my mind and cannot
gain entrance to my thought. I am happy, well, and
filled with perfect life. I live in the Spirit of Truth and
am conscious that the Spirit of Truth lives in me. My

word is the law unto its own manifestation, and will bring me, or cause me to be brought, to its fulfillment. There is no unbelief, no doubt, no uncertainty. I know, and I know that I know. Let every thought of doubt vanish from my mind, that I may know the Truth and the Truth may make me free. (End.)

A PERSONAL PRAYER

I pray that love and all of its gifts may come into your life. I pray that you will see more of love, peace, freedom and security in your life every day. I pray that you will see that you do not get those gifts by "going on a hunt for them," but by learning to "feel" them as they are <u>now</u> in you, and in the world around you.

I pray you will read as much as you can about the great gifts that we have investigated together. And I pray that whatever you do or do not do, love, peace, freedom and security will grow quickly and plainly in your life and mind.

In the Most Holy Name of Jesus, who actually <u>is</u> LOVE, Amen.
A. D. G.

Section Fourteen
Goals And Means

Now that we have again looked through the codes at the entire universe, let me remind you of the intentions in this book.

We wished, with your cooperation, to sneak certain positive concepts and "feelings" past your conscious mind into your subconscious mind. The goal was to set up favorable conditions for the detection, retention, and nurturing of, the great gifts of love, peace, freedom, and security. We said that love is the greatest, all-inclusive gift, which actually contains, and is really the source of all other possible, desirable gifts.

We said that love is not a commodity. It cannot be bought, stolen, or given to you. Being rich, famous, having great power, being incredibly strong or very intelligent, will not help you at all to gain love. The poor, weak and unknown person is, here, on a level playing-field with everybody else.

So, we proposed a means to experience a reality that is not material, as we usually think of material things. We reaffirmed that love is not arrived at by intellectual processes. It must be experienced "as it somehow comes to you, and is enjoyed within."

Because of that, we asked you, as much as possible, to stop thinking all together in your reading. We asked you to try to "feel" under the words of this book, which, at least in theory, is easier if you suspend thought and read everything only passively.

We said that "soulmates" are real. We said that a person can have one, and only one, soulmate, and that the greatest joy in love for anyone is realized in union with that soulmate. We said that such unions are rare, as reflected in the statements of Emanuel Swedenborg about this.

That is why pairings of couples through compatibility profiles, counselors and trials of companionship are useful. But such unions are always second-best to soulmate unions, although they can be pleasant, functional, and productive in ordinary human terms.

Meanwhile, our "nonthinking" look into love and its gifts was used to "feel into" the very internal areas in all of us where love can be most fully experienced. The idea was that learning about those deeper areas, which our busy lives usually prevent us from sensing, makes it easier for love to enter into us.

You want love, and love wants you. If you learn of love's nature, and do what you can to become receptive to love, it is more likely that it will find a home within you. And the process of gaining love, since it is not something you can "go out and grab," always requires that love should enter you.

So, repeating, we asked you to use our "sneaky," method of learning about love and about where love most "loves to live," because we wish to have love in order to be happy. And love is not only the entire component of happiness, it is also, as we said before, the giver of value to everything in the universe.

Keep working, then, to open yourself to the entry of love. For once you truly love, you will be immunized forever against feeling pain in not being loved. You will have the key to <u>everything</u>.

As we phrased this, before, possessing true love places you in the very center of all knowledge, understandings, meanings, and values.

You are no longer on the outside, looking in.

You have arrived.

You are on the inside, looking out.

And this is the end of my book.

(Please look at the booklist in the next section, my statements about it, and about how reading some or all of the books listed could increase the usefulness of this book to you.)

Section Fifteen
Reading Suggestions

Below are some explanatory notes. Following them, is a list of books which contain some of the ideas and evidences relevant to the subject matter in this writing.

There are many reasons to read unusual books like those listed. The main reason is to bring into mind some concepts that are different from those hammered into us by the everyday world. Most everyday ideas are so matter-oriented and pessimistic that they tend to wear down our will-power and optimism. Those negative effects need to be counteracted.

You get the messages of the world without asking for them. They come to us every waking moment. We often dream about them. We feel the battering effects of worldly affairs on us every hour of the day.

We have a defense to all of the negativism. We find writing that is not so worldly and gloomy. We should read such writing. You are not likely to find ideas like those in the listed books in anybody that you normally meet. And as you read, you begin to recognize less earthy phenomena in other people and things.

These books will show you reasons to be cheerful that workaday life hides from you; reasons that almost all deny by their usual actions and speech. The books will open your mind to other possible ways of speaking and acting.

The physical world cuts and bruises us every day. We are liable to pain and death through many kinds of accident. The world disturbs us with noises, itchings and burnings, frustrated appetites and needs. Often it is too hot or too cold, too fast or too slow, there is too much water or not enough, too much attention from others, or too little. Make your own long list.

But in the suggested books there are levels of thinking that can stop many of the bad effects of physical events, and increase the good effects. These levels of thinking can sometimes free you completely from physical conditions in the ordinary sense.

One such book gives a medical approach to making life easier and happier. This is Dr. Schindler's "How To Live 365 Days A Year." Dr. Carrell's "Man The Unknown," also attempts to advance happiness, but in a somewhat different way.

Another book is the life story of a man who showed great psychic powers. That is "Edgar Cayce, The Sleeping Prophet," by Jess Stearn. You will find that many books of this kind are well-documented. Most are written by reliable and honest reporters about honest and trustworthy people.

One book is by the distinguished American psychologist and philosopher, William James. Its title is "William James On Psychical Research." The book describes his controlled sessions of study of a psychic known as Mrs. Piper. She was being studied by "The American Society For Psychical Research." This study continued for many years. The report seems to give evidence for some sort of life after death. Dr. James states the facts of this investigation, then offers his opinions as to what the facts may mean.

Some books give systems of moral behavior that have been built up through thousands of years by people who report what they believe are personal insights or revelations of spiritual realities. "First Principles of Theosophy," by C. Jinarajadasa is such a book. It has many interesting diagrams and pictures in it. The book also shows the immense periods of time that Hindu philosophers and sages have always thought must pass as worlds and life grow.

There are books written through mediums by persons who were formerly alive on earth but dead at the time of the sittings. Seemingly, though, the mind, or some psychic "leftover" of each person gave out the text of various books. A book like this is "The Unobstructed Universe," given by Patricia

White through a personal friend as medium, to her husband. One book that apparently describes soulmate pairs is "Lovers, Nymphs and Other Maniacs," by Hal Wallace, although, I believe, Mr. Wallace does not mention the term "soulmates" in the stories or in any asides.

Some of the listed books give more mechanical, or, more "mechanical-looking," ways of trying to tap into a plane of power and happenings above or within the material world. These books describe astrology, fortune-telling by using cards, tea leaves or sticks and bones, almost anything that can produce patterns or some observed order of objects. The title of such a book will usually identify the system. You may have already read this type of book. If so, read more. The books are expansive to the mind.

But the persons I want most of all to read a few of these books are those who have not read any of them, or persons who may not know if they have ever read anything like them.

Each book should be read like any book of information; with an open mind. But decide how much you feel you can trust the reporter, or whoever is the source, of the material. You will find it unlikely that any of the informants, here, are abnormal, dishonest, or "just in it for the money." All try hard to be objective and factual. Almost all are very convincing.

The first suggested book, already mentioned, is "How To Live 365 Days A Year," by Dr. John Schindler. This book offers insights into the mind-base of the health of the body. Dr. Schindler argues that the rules of philosophy, religion and mysticism work for the same reasons that a doctor's advice works.

The second book is "Edgar Cayce, The Sleeping Prophet." Edgar Cayce was a psychic for whose doings there is an amazing amount of proof.

Third, is the autobiography of the medium, Arthur Ford, "Nothing So Strange." In it, Mr. Ford tells how he found his "powers," and what those powers mean for life.

The last of the first four most-recommended books is another book by Jess Stearn, "The Search For The Girl With The Blue Eyes." It describes an apparent instance of reincarnation, "the girl with the blue eyes" being the example.

I advance these four books first because they deal with very interesting and unusual events, and are also easier going for first readings than some of the others. They are examples of somewhat mystical reading, and will surprise many who do not know of this kind of material.

Now, the booklist. These, I believe, go from the easiest to the more difficult.

How To Live 365 Days A Year .. Dr. John A. Schindler

Edgar Cayce, The Sleeping Prophet . . Jess Stearn

Nothing So Strange . . . . Arthur Ford

The Search For The Girl With The Blue Eyes . . . .
Jess Stearn

The Other Side . . . . Bishop James Pike

Man The Unknown . . . . Dr. Alexis Carrell

Here And Hereafter . . . . Ruth Montgomery

Many Lives Many Loves . . . . . Dr. Gina Cerminara

Many Voices . . . . Eileen Garrett

The World Beyond . . . . Ruth Montgomery

The Unobstructed Universe . . . . Patricia White

William James On Psychical Research . . . .
William James

The Unaccountable . . . . Dr. Nandor Fodor

The Psychic World Of Peter Hurkos . . . .
Norma Lee Browning

Astrology: The Space Age Science . . . .
Joseph F. Goodavage

Astrological Digest On Love, Sex, Marriage. . . Zolar

The Secret Of The Ages . . . . Robert Collier

Human Personality And Its Survival of Bodily Death . . .
F. W. H. Myers

Cosmic Consciousness . . . .
Richard Maurice Bucke, M. D.

The Miracle Of The Ages . . . . . . Browne Landowne

First Principles Of Theosophy . . . . . C. Jinarajadasa

The Morning Of The Magicians . . . . . Louis Pauwels
and Jacques Bergier

Uni-Chotometrics, A New Way Of Life . . . .
Eugene A. Albright

Encyclopedia Of Astrology . . . . . . Nicholas DeVore

I list the "Encyclopedia of Astrology" so that you may read the article beginning on page 229, <u>The Invariable Plane</u>. See also, on page 231, at the bottom, the interesting discussion of modern astronomy's confirmation of the Hindu Great Age, called the Mahayuga, as the period of return of all the planets (then known) in our solar system to the same positions relative to one another. The duration of a Mahayuga and the period of actual return both equal 4,320,000 years.

On page 233 of the Encyclopedia of Astrology, in the same <u>Invariable Plane</u> article, is a discussion of the multiple cross-relationships of the plane with the planets and stars at the time of Christ's birth. These relationships, confirmed by astronomy, could not have happened at any time in the <u>last</u> two <u>billion</u> years of earth history, and <u>cannot</u> happen again for <u>another</u> two <u>billion</u> years.

Again, anyone who is not familiar with this kind of information will find it very interesting to read at least a few books on the list.

May Love be yours forever, my friend.

I pray also that you will be forever happy.

Albert David Griffith